WHAT PEOPLE ARE SAYING...

Most emotional intelligence books explain the concept—this one helps you use it. The Emotional Intelligence Playbook is a practical, scenario-based guide designed for anyone navigating tricky workplace dynamics. Instead of abstract theory, you'll get real-world situations, step-by-step tools, and a repeatable success model to help you respond (not react) in the moments that matter most.

—Silvia Gorla, PhD, Psychologist

Captivating vignettes highlight interpersonal dilemmas through brief and focused dialogues written with the keen insight of a screenwriter. The book provides strategies for resolving common roadblocks in daily communications. Fun, engaging, and instructive – a book worth buying and saving for reference when life's journeys require a different approach and mindset.

—Christina Knox, College Educator

This book turns the often esoteric concept of Emotional Intelligence into easily understandable, tangible, actionable, bite-sized chunks for self-improvement. Each chapter creates an individualized cheat sheet for faster learning.

—Dr. Suzanne Ames, President, Peninsula College

THE EMOTIONAL INTELLIGENCE PLAYBOOK

TRANSFORM YOUR CAREER WITH STRATEGIES AND SCENARIOS FOR WORKPLACE SUCCESS

BARBARA A. KERR

BARBARA A. KERR PRESS

mon ami, toujours

Copyright © 2025 by Barbara A. Kerr

All rights reserved.

Cover design by Jennifer Stimson

ISBN: 979-8-9989887-1-4

No part of this book may be reproduced in any form or by any electronic or mechanical means, including information storage and retrieval systems, without written permission from the author, except for the use of brief quotations in a book review.

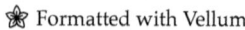 Formatted with Vellum

"The secret of health for both mind and body is not to mourn for the past, not to worry about the future, but to live the present moment wisely and earnestly."

The Buddha

CHAPTER 1
YOU ARE INVITED: STEP INTO REAL-WORLD EMOTIONAL INTELLIGENCE

Step into the shoes of six professionals facing real-world workplace conflicts. Whether you see yourself in their struggles or recognize someone you know, each scenario challenges you to think critically about Emotional Intelligence (EI).

Walk alongside these characters and observe their difficulties, discoveries, joys, and accomplishments. Each character's journey to greater EI is told through dramatic, real-life scenarios involving conflict at work, and sometimes at home. As you read, you'll be invited to imagine how you would resolve these situations and make decisions. Then, track each character's EI progress along the way.

Start by choosing a character who speaks to you, or dive in from the beginning to experience their stories as they unfold. However you begin, you'll discover practical lessons, coaching tips, and fresh perspectives to help you grow your Emotional Intelligence.

CHAPTER 2
WHAT IS EMOTIONAL INTELLIGENCE AND WHY CARE ABOUT IT?

The workplace continues to evolve—remote work, collaborative teams, more women in leadership, the rise of personal and professional coaching, and the introduction of AI are just a few changes shaping the 21st century. Yet one thing remains constant: emotions are always in the room.

Whether you're leading a team meeting, working solo on a creative project, or managing a high-stakes Zoom call, emotions shape how you think, connect, and perform. Navigating your own feelings—and understanding those of others—is central to success.

That's where Emotional Intelligence (EI) comes in.

EI is your internal navigation system for emotional life. Like a GPS guiding you through city streets or hiking trails, EI helps you stay oriented through workplace challenges and unexpected turns. It doesn't prevent conflict, but it enables you to chart a course through it.

THE SUCCESS MODEL

In this book, the *Success Model of Emotional Intelligence* is used as a reference point to indicate the growth of characters' EI—in the Progress Tracker at the end of each scenario.

Emotional Intelligence in action means applying the five key dimensions:

- Self-Awareness
- Actions of the Self
- Awareness of Others
- Interaction with Others
- Resilience.

The graphic below indicates these five interrelated aspects of Emotional Intelligence. The good news is that you can enhance your skills —if you're willing to learn and practice.

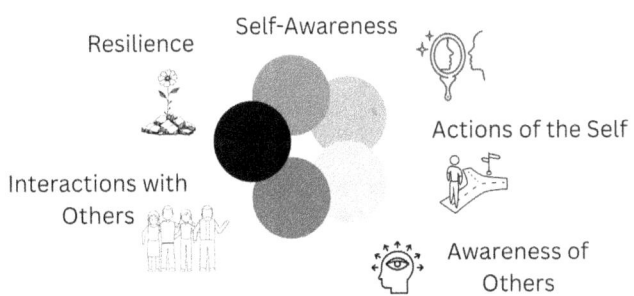

THE SUCCESS MODEL of EMOTIONAL INTELLIGENCE

This model outlines five key dimensions of Emotional Intelligence that support personal success. Each dimension is defined below, along with examples of how it manifests in everyday behavior. Use this section as a reference to recognize and strengthen these skills in yourself.

SELF-AWARENESS

Self-Awareness is understanding your own emotions, strengths, values, and motivations. It means paying attention to your inner state and recognizing how your thoughts and feelings influence your actions. Someone with strong self-awareness frequently reflects on personal experiences to learn and grow. An individual with strong Self-Awareness:

- Pauses to notice feelings and thoughts before reacting
- Clearly identifies emotions and what triggers them
- Recognizes personal strengths and limitations in various situations
- Reflects on how beliefs and values shape choices and actions
- Pays attention to feedback from others to understand how one is perceived

ACTIONS OF THE SELF

Actions of the Self describe how you manage and act on your self-awareness. It involves regulating emotions and behaviors to align with your values and goals. In practice, this means taking deliberate steps to maintain balance and achieve your goals. An individual skilled in this dimension:

- Treats oneself with compassion and understanding, even after mistakes
- Regulates emotions to stay calm and balanced under pressure

- Expresses feelings and needs clearly and appropriately to others
- Plans ahead and sets realistic goals to handle challenges proactively
- Holds oneself accountable by honoring commitments and personal standards

AWARENESS OF OTHERS

Awareness of Others is the ability to perceive and understand the emotions, needs, and perspectives of people around you. It builds on self-awareness and involves paying attention to social cues. With strong awareness of others, you sense unspoken concerns and recognize how people feel in different situations. An individual who is strong in Awareness of Others:

- Observes body language, tone of voice, and facial expressions to gauge feelings
- Listens actively and empathetically, seeking to understand others' viewpoints
- Notices when someone may need support or is being left out
- Detects underlying emotions in conversations beyond the words spoken
- Respects differences by considering others' backgrounds and experiences

INTERACTION WITH OTHERS

Interaction with Others is about using your awareness to connect effectively and build meaningful relationships. It encompasses communication, cooperation, and conflict resolution. People skilled in this dimension create trust and collaboration by applying empathy and respect in their dealings with others. An individual who is skilled in Interaction with Others:

- Communicates openly and respectfully, encouraging honest dialogue
- Collaborates by inviting input, valuing others' ideas, and sharing credit
- Resolves conflicts constructively, focusing on mutual understanding and solutions
- Builds trust through consistency, support, and keeping promises
- Inspires and motivates people by showing genuine interest and appreciation

RESILIENCE

Resilience is the ability to recover from setbacks and adapt to change while maintaining a positive outlook. It means learning from mistakes and persisting toward goals despite challenges. Resilient individuals remain flexible, hopeful, and determined even in difficult circumstances.

- Bounces back from difficulties by viewing setbacks as learning opportunities
- Maintains an optimistic mindset and looks for silver linings in problems
- Adjusts plans and stays flexible when facing unexpected obstacles
- Perseveres with determination, staying focused on long-term goals
- Practices self-care and seeks support when needed to sustain energy and well-being

CHAPTER 3
YOUR INNER GPS: WHAT EMOTIONAL INTELLIGENCE CAN DO FOR YOU

If you find it helpful to use analogies for understanding abstract ideas, think of Emotional Intelligence as your *inner GPS*. Just as a GPS helps you navigate roads or trails, recalculating in real time when you veer off course, Emotional Intelligence helps you steer through the emotional ups and downs of work and life.

EI doesn't prevent conflict or discomfort, but it gives you tools to respond with greater clarity and purpose.

GPS AND EI COMPARISON

GPS: Helps you identify your current position.

EI: **Helps** *you identify emotions as they arise.*

GPS: Prompts you to identify your destination.

EI: **Helps** *you consider options and decide on the desired outcomes in a given situation.*

GPS: Recognizes obstacles in the environment or errors on the part of the user.

*EI: **Helps** you learn from mistakes or "failure" as you work to resolve an issue.*

GPS: Recalculates new routes to your destination without drama, blame, or guilt.

*EI: **Helps** you quickly get back on a course to bring success without drama, blame, or guilt.*

GPS: Helps you reach your intended destination despite obstacles.

*EI: **Helps** you accept the inevitable changes in the environment and achieve your desired outcomes.*

Just like with a GPS, you won't always have the perfect map, but EI helps you adjust, reflect, and reroute when needed.

In the pages ahead, you'll walk alongside six characters as they learn to listen to their *inner GPS*. As their stories unfold, you'll gain insight into how Emotional Intelligence shows up in everyday decisions, large and small. You'll also begin to observe your own emotional navigation system—and how it can grow stronger with awareness and practice.

CHAPTER 4
WHAT TO EXPECT

You'll follow six characters through a series of real-life conflicts—some internal, some interpersonal. In each scenario, you'll explore how they wrestle with tough choices, take action, and gradually build their Emotional Intelligence.

Each chapter follows the same structure to guide your reflection:

SCENARIO

A brief snapshot of a conflict in the workplace—or occasionally at home—that puts the character's Emotional Intelligence to the test

WHAT WOULD YOU THINK?

Step into the character's perspective. What thoughts or assumptions are shaping their reaction?

NEXT STEP

See what the character chooses to do next. Would you take the same approach?

COACHING TIPS

Practical, actionable guidance for handling similar situations in your own life

REFLECTION

A moment to pause. What resonates with your own experiences or challenges?

PROGRESS TRACKER

A summary of the Emotional Intelligence skills the character begins to develop, linked to the five dimensions of the *Success Model*

Here's an example of a Progress Tracker entry:

———

Self-Awareness:

✅ Becomes more aware of how colleagues perceive them

Awareness of Others:

✅ Understands that others feel disrespected when not truly heard

———

Before you jump into the first scenario, take a moment to meet the players: **Susan, Jake, Marjorie, Anthony, Emily, and Juan.** Each one brings a different background, temperament, and workplace setting—from healthcare and education to law, retail, non-profit, and corporate leadership. No one is perfect, but all are learning to navigate conflict with more Emotional Intelligence.

Each scenario becomes part of your Emotional Intelligence "map," strengthening your inner GPS.

CHAPTER 5
MEET THE CHARACTERS

SUSAN – THE DEDICATED NURSE

Susan is a skilled and compassionate nurse in a busy hospital. While she excels at patient care, she struggles with self-advocacy and setting boundaries. Over time, she learns to manage workplace stress, navigate tough conversations, and stand up for herself without losing her warmth.

Fun Fact: Susan loves tending her garden while listening to recorded whale songs—a quiet counterbalance to hospital chaos.

JAKE – THE SMART BUT SOCIALLY CLUELESS LEGAL INTERN

Jake

Jake is brilliant but arrogant—poor at listening and teamwork. Through missteps and growth, he begins to transform from a know-it-all into a genuine connector.

Fun Fact: Jake has traded video games for espionage thrillers—he still loves strategy, just with more heart.

MARJORIE – THE HIGH-PRESSURE RETAIL MANAGER

MARJORIE

Marjorie runs a prestigious department store's shoe division with precision and drive. But her tough management style alienates her team. Emotional Intelligence enables her to lead with greater insight and compassion.

Fun Fact: Marjorie finds solace in musicals, where even high drama finds harmony.

ANTHONY – THE VISIONARY EXECUTIVE (WITH A SHARP EDGE)

ANTHONY

Anthony is decisive and ambitious but often bulldozes others in pursuit of results. His journey reveals the value of Emotional Intelligence in becoming a truly inspiring leader.

Fun Fact: Anthony is taking his family on a two-week sea turtle protection project—an unexpected path toward empathy.

EMILY – THE OVERWORKED NON-PROFIT ADMIN ASSISTANT

EMILY

Emily juggles nonstop responsibilities and often feels invisible. EI helps her advocate for herself, set boundaries, and stay true to her mission without burning out.

Fun Fact: Emily finds balance in the fast, focused world of snowboarding, where carving her own path is key.

JUAN – THE IT DEAN WHO MEANS BUSINESS

JUAN

Juan, a no-nonsense community college IT dean, prides himself on efficiency. But his blunt leadership style creates friction. He learns to balance expectations with empathy and improve team communication.

Fun Fact: Juan's birdwatching hobby teaches him patience—something he's learning to apply at work, too.

CHAPTER 6
SUSAN

Follow Susan's progress in learning to approach conflict with Emotional Intelligence as she interacts with patients, patients' families, and coworkers. Watch as Susan begins to understand her own pursuit of perfection, sets healthier boundaries, and gradually reclaims her emotional wellbeing.

SUSAN'S SCENARIOS

- Superhero Boundaries
- Under Pressure
- Emotional Energy Drain
- Why Beat Yourself Up?
- Not So Fast
- Human Kindness

CHAPTER 7
SUPERHERO BOUNDARIES

Our boundaries define our personal space--and we need to be sovereign there in order to be able to step into our full power and potential.

JESSICA MOORE

SCENARIO

Timmy, an eight-year-old, is a patient at a large urban hospital. He is recovering from injuries after a terrible car accident. The nursing staff is becoming increasingly exasperated with his attitude and ask for Susan's help.

Susan enters Timmy's room. His lunch tray is untouched. He is staring at the television.

Susan: Hi, Timmy, I'm nurse Susie. I've heard that you are having a tough day. Perhaps I can help.

Timmy: No way! You just want to change my bandages, and I'm not gonna let you or anyone. Leave me alone!

Susan: You're right, Timmy. I'd like to see those bandages changed. But I promise you--I won't do anything without your permission. Let's take a break for a minute. Would you be willing to play a game with me?

Timmy: (*reluctantly*) What kind of game?

Susan: It's a game I played with my little brother when he was just about your age. We pretended we had superpowers! If you could have one superpower, what would it be?

Timmy: (*brief smile*) That's easy. Teleportation.

Susan: (*laughs*) Ah, of course--you're pretty quick, Timmy. And if you could teleport anywhere right now, where would you go?

Timmy: (*sighs*) I'd go to the park near my home and ride my bike like lightning through the woods.

Susan: Got it! Now here's the game. We can pretend to go bike riding in the park while nurse Jennie changes your bandages. You have the power to transport me there with you, right?

Timmy: Maybe . . . but only for five minutes.

Susan: That should be plenty of time. Thanks for being so brave, Timmy.

WHAT WOULD YOU THINK?

Susan may feel torn as she interacts with Tommy. Can you place yourself in her shoes? Consider:

Emotionally Reactive Thoughts:

I'm at the end of a twelve-hour shift, and I'm exhausted. But I feel for this poor little kid. And Jennie really needs my help managing the situation. I don't want to let her and the other nurses down.

Emotionally Intelligent Thoughts:

I love helping kids, but I'm running on empty. I've got to find another way or I'll burn out--just like the others.

SUSAN'S NEXT STEP

We can choose our thoughts to guide our actions. See what you think of Susan's choice:

———

If I don't make a change, I'll burn out. At our next staff meeting, I plan to suggest something I learned about at a recent conference: establishing peer support groups where we can find strength in one another and learn to manage the stressful and challenging situations we face.

———

COACHING TIPS

Taking on others' suffering and stress too intensely can be damaging and lead to less effective outcomes. We can manage our boundaries and still be kind and compassionate to others.

☑ **Acknowledge Your Stress:** Headaches, other body aches, fatigue, and depression are some of the signs that you are under undue stress. What causes negative feelings and stress in your life?

☑ **Define Limits and Set Boundaries:** Healthy boundaries are identified through strong self-awareness, especially being clear about what you value.

☑ **Respond with Emotional Intelligence:** Your compassion and care can be expressed without ignoring your own needs-- offering new ideas for solutions, for example, or finding new ways to handle stressful situations with more support.

REFLECTION

- How would defining a boundary bring less stress to your life?

PROGRESS TRACKER: USING THE SUCCESS MODEL

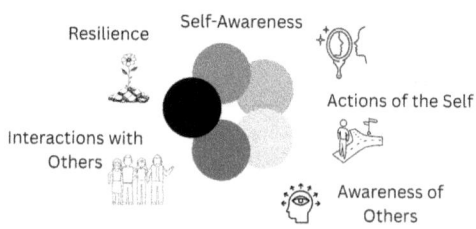

THE SUCCESS MODEL of EMOTIONAL INTELLIGENCE

Self-Awareness

☑ Realizes that stress affects not only her mood, it's showing up in how she communicates with colleagues

Actions of the Self

☑ Takes proactive steps to manage stress—setting boundaries, scheduling short breaks, and acknowledging when she needs support

CHAPTER 8
UNDER PRESSURE

The greatest weapon against stress is our ability to choose one thought over another.

—WILLIAM JAMES

SCENARIO

Susan is taking vitals on an elderly hospital patient when the patient's son, Jack Farley, angrily confronts her.

Jack: Have you nurses gotten my mother up and walking yet?

Susan: Not yet, but we're . . .

Jack: (*loudly*) Her doctor said it was vital that she be up within twelve hours of her surgery. It's past time!

Susan: Your mother was a bit slow in recovering from the anesthesia and pain meds--not unusual at her age. She may be able . . .

Jack: (*more loudly*) When is the doctor visiting her again? I want to speak with him. Why aren't you nurses following his orders?

WHAT WOULD YOU THINK?

Susan may feel herself growing angry, red-faced, hands shaking perhaps, as Jack pressures her for answers. At the same time, she may be feeling compassion for this patient's son. Consider:

Emotionally Reactive Thoughts:

Hold on a minute, buddy. You don't need to tell me how to do my job. I've spent years in training and have cared for thousands of patients like your mother. Don't insult me and let me do my job!

Emotionally Intelligent Thoughts:

You must be worried about your mom. No one wants to see their mother lying helpless in a hospital bed. How can I bring some calm to this situation?

SUSAN'S NEXT STEP

We can choose our thoughts to guide our actions. See what you think of Susan's choice:

———

"I understand your concern, Mr. Farley. We've got her care covered, and now that she's stable, we'll get her walking. You can come with us and chat with her."

———

COACHING TIPS

When you're under some external pressure, managing your emotions can be especially challenging.

THE EMOTIONAL INTELLIGENCE PLAYBOOK

✅ **Stop the Train!** Take a deep breath, pause, and remind yourself of your goal: to de-escalate the situation and find a mutually agreeable solution.

✅ **Empathize:** Find that understanding that you would have had if you had not been under pressure. Be in touch with your values.

✅ **Respond with Emotional Intelligence:** By managing your frustration and anger, you gain the power to not only de-escalate the situation but to find a creative solution.

REFLECTION

- How do you handle your emotions when under pressure from someone like Mr. Farley?

PROGRESS TRACKER: USING THE SUCCESS MODEL

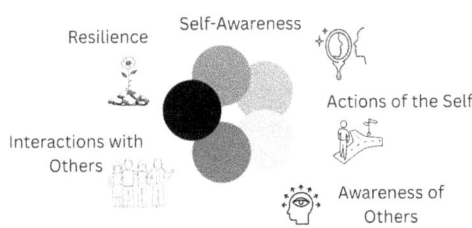

THE SUCCESS MODEL of EMOTIONAL INTELLIGENCE

Self-Awareness

✅Begins to shift from immediate frustration to pausing before responding, leading to more thoughtful communication

Actions of the Self

☑Stays calm under pressure and listens without escalating to understand and empathize with others' emotions. Finds a way to calm herself and identify a satisfying resolution to the conflict

CHAPTER 9
EMOTIONAL ENERGY DRAIN

Setting boundaries is not about pushing people away; it's about protecting your energy, creating space for healthy relationships, and ensuring people respect your needs.

HENRY CLOUD

SCENARIO

Susan sits on a bench under her favorite tree in the courtyard outside the hospital. She eats a salad and listens to calming music on her AirPods.

Another nurse, Sylvia, wanders out to the courtyard.

Sylvia: Do you mind if I join you, Susan? Beautiful day, eh?

Susan smiles and removes her AirPods.

Sylvia: I just had to get some air. I'm sick and tired of being treated like dirt!

Susan: More problems with Dr. Meyer?

Sylvia: He gives me orders without even looking me in the eye. And never a word of thanks.

Susan: I get it, and I'm sorry. That's hard to put up with.

Sylvia: I had everything set to give a patient a sponge bath when he appeared for a visit. Like his time is so much more important than mine.

WHAT WOULD YOU THINK?

Susan finds herself in a familiar dilemma. How can she kindly acknowledge her friend's frustration but also protect her peace? Consider:

Emotionally Reactive Thoughts:

Can I just have fifteen minutes to eat my lunch in peace? Do you think you're the only one with issues? You can't just dump your emotions on me all the time.

Emotionally Intelligent Thoughts:

We've been over this so often--Dr. Meyer is a jerk--I quite agree. But if I let Sylvia keep venting to me, I start to feel the effects of her negativity. How can I stop her complaining without being mean?

SUSAN'S NEXT STEP

We can choose our thoughts to guide our actions. What do you think of Susan's choice?

> **"I hear you, Sylvia. I know Dr. Meyer can be frustrating, but I really need this break to reset. Let's catch up later."**

COACHING TIPS

If you are an empathetic person, you may find yourself serving as a "dumping ground" for someone's negativity. That presents a dilemma--wanting to be kind while also preserving your peace.

✅ **Be Honest:** If someone's venting is overwhelming you with negativity or perhaps triggering unpleasant memories, acknowledge that--to yourself and to the person who is venting. Being honest doesn't have to be unkind: "I'm not in a good place to listen right now."

✅ **Establish a Boundary:** Listen with empathy when it is appropriate, but know when it is time to set a clear boundary with someone who repeatedly vents to you.

✅ **Respond with Emotional Intelligence:** Initiate a straightforward conversation with the complainer, first by validating their experience, but then explaining how their venting about this issue affects you.

REFLECTION

- What would you have said to Sylvia to stop her venting to you so you could maintain your peace?

PROGRESS TRACKER: USING THE SUCCESS MODEL

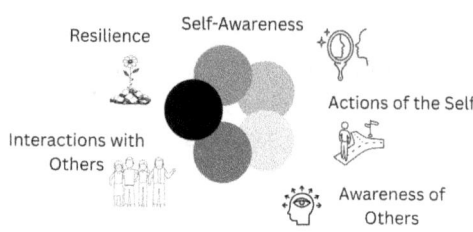

THE SUCCESS MODEL of EMOTIONAL INTELLIGENCE

Self-Awareness

✅ Identifies her internal struggle between wanting to help a friend and protecting her peace of mind.

Actions of the Self

✅ Gently acknowledges her coworker's emotions with her body language (smile) and words of understanding

✅ Realizes the need for self-care and sets a firm boundary, but balances that with a plan to help her coworker.

CHAPTER 10
WHY BEAT YOURSELF UP?

Stop beating yourself up, and leave insecurity behind.

BRENE BROWN

SCENARIO

It is just after midnight. Susan sits at a kitchen counter, an empty pint container of caramel cone ice cream in front of her.

Susan: *I should have remembered to put notes on that patient's chart. How did I forget?*

Susan's inner voice: *You're obsessing about this as usual. You were crazy busy at the time--remember? It was a minor mistake.*

Susan: *But I don't want to make mistakes. Not even "minor" ones. That's not who I am!*

Susan's inner voice: *You know that's ridiculous. You're not superhuman. Everyone makes mistakes.*

WHAT WOULD YOU THINK?

Self-reflection—demonstrated here in Susan's late-night self-talk—can sometimes reveal to us things that were hidden from our awareness. Consider:

Emotionally Reactive Thoughts:

What if everyone knows about my mistake? I can't get it out of my mind. Am I just pathetic?

Emotionally Intelligent Thoughts:

Why am I beating myself up over this? This was an oversight, an error that anyone could make. The problem lies within my own mind, not in reality.

SUSAN'S NEXT STEP

We can choose our thoughts to guide our actions. See what you think of Susan's choice:

"I will let go of this issue and learn from my mistake. I can accept that it is normal to make errors. Although that sounds so obvious, it's actually a big step forward for me!"

☑ **Go Easy:** Instead of beating yourself up, remind yourself that your mistakes do not define you.

☑ **Find the Lesson and the Remedy:** How could this error or similar errors be avoided in the future?

☑ **Respond with Emotional Intelligence:** Accept that you are human--a good human, but like all humans, apt to make mistakes.

REFLECTION

- What would you say to a friend who made the same mistake?
- Who would you be if you made zero mistakes?

PROGRESS TRACKER: USING THE SUCCESS MODEL

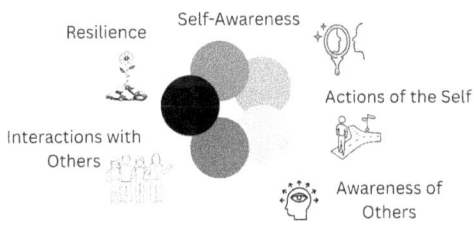

THE SUCCESS MODEL of EMOTIONAL INTELLIGENCE

Self-Awareness

☑ Acknowledges her tendency to be unrealistic in striving for perfection

☑ Becomes aware that her imagination is overtaking the reality of the situation, causing her even greater stress

Actions of the Self

☑ Acknowledges that making mistakes is normal

☑ Makes a conscious decision to "let go" of blaming herself when she makes a mistake

CHAPTER 11
NOT SO FAST

Perfectionism is internalized oppression.

GLORIA STEINEM

SCENARIO

Susan is on a break, sitting in the hospital cafeteria across from Eleanor, a nursing supervisor. It has been a long day.

Eleanor: You're an excellent nurse, Susan. The doctors depend on you. The patients love you. Your notes are clear and complete. You never complain, and you never stop moving! All that makes it hard for me to say what I want to say to you.

Susan: (*sipping a cup of tea*) Please--just tell me. Have I done something wrong? Something to make you angry?

Eleanor: No, no. Nothing wrong, my dear. This is just a little unsolicited advice--forgive me--from an old nurse who has been around for a long time. I'm saying it to be helpful.

Susan: I don't understand . . .

Eleanor: (*reaches out to touch Susan's arm*) You try so hard to make everything just right, and you expect everyone else to care as much as you do. What you're doing is like cooking a five-course meal by yourself--something's gonna burn! I don't want to see that happen to you.

WHAT WOULD YOU THINK?

Sometimes we are brought to self-awareness through another person—a coach, a friend, a therapist. This may be the first time Susan questions her definition of "excellence." Her initial reaction is to defend herself and reject the friend's advice. Consider:

Emotionally Reactive Thoughts:

But I'm just doing my job--excellently, as she has pointed out! How can she criticize me for having high standards and for working hard? Does she really want me to begin doing sloppy work or cutting corners? I'm proud of my accomplishments.

Emotionally Intelligent Thoughts:

Is this true? Is this how other people see me--as Little Miss Perfect--like my brothers used to tease me? That was just about grades or my outfits. This is more serious, and Eleanor is giving me a heartfelt warning.

SUSAN'S NEXT STEP

We can choose our thoughts to guide our actions. See what you think of Susan's choice:

I thought perfection was my strength. But maybe it's holding me back. How do I let go of pursuing perfection and feel that what I'm doing is "good enough?

COACHING TIPS

We sometimes hold on to our habitual ways of thinking and action by saying, "That's just how I am," unable or unwilling to consider that those thoughts and behaviors may be harmful to us. But if some aspect of our inner life surfaces to our self-awareness, the next step is figuring out what action to take.

☑ **Recognize the Downside:** If we recognize that what we've been holding on to has negative consequences, we can take action to modify our attitude and behavior.

☑ **Discover the Secret of "Good Enough:"** This discovery may take some serious self-talk to admit that you are human, to give yourself permission to make mistakes and take some risks, and to leave behind the pursuit of perfection.

☑ **Respond with Emotional Intelligence:** Reach out for help if necessary--a coach, perhaps--who can help you improve your relationship with yourself for an authentic and satisfying life.

REFLECTION

- How was Susan's "excellent" performance as a nurse affecting her life?
- What has perfection cost you?

PROGRESS TRACKER: USING THE SUCCESS MODEL

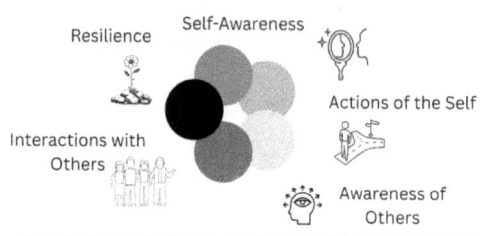

THE SUCCESS MODEL of EMOTIONAL INTELLIGENCE

Self-Awareness

☑ Notices her tendency to react defensively when criticized

Actions of the Self

☑ Shifts her understanding of "perfection" to acknowledge that the pursuit of perfection can lead to negative consequences

CHAPTER 12
HUMAN KINDNESS

Never say 'yes' with your lips, if in your heart you are saying 'no.'

PAOLO COELHO

SCENARIO

It is Friday evening after work. Susan is meeting her boyfriend, Bror, for a beer at a neighborhood bar.

Bror: Hey--good news, sweetie! I found a great little Airbnb just a block from the beach in Redondo Beach. This means sunshine and some well-deserved relaxation for us.

Susan: Ah! I've been dreaming of lying on the beach in the sunshine and listening to the waves! But a little problem has come up, and I'm not sure what to do.

Bror: I thought the hospital schedule was all set . . .

Susan: It was, I mean, it is--but Cynthia's mother, who is in a nursing home, fell and broke her hip, and she--

Bror: Wait, don't tell me--she asked you to take her shift again!

Susan: I don't want to let Cynthia down... but I really need this break.

Bror: And you deserve it.

WHAT WOULD YOU THINK?

Old habits die hard, as the saying goes. Although Susan understands the importance of self-care, she may still fall back on her desire to be needed. Consider:

Emotionally Reactive Thoughts:

Poor Cynthia, she's beside herself. I hate to disappoint her. I don't know who will take her shift if I say no. I don't want to disappoint Bror either. I don't know what to do.

Emotionally Intelligent Thoughts:

Bror has been trying to convince me for months to get some R&R because of all the stress at the hospital. I know he's right. I need to take care of myself and take a break from other people's problems.

SUSAN'S NEXT STEP

We can choose our thoughts to guide our actions. See what you think of Susan's choice:

By taking care of myself, taking a break from non-stop stress, I will have more energy and motivation for my job as well as a healthier balance in my personal life.

COACHING TIPS

✅ **Consider Priorities:** Protecting yourself from external stresses — often the demands and needs of others — should be high on your list of priorities.

✅ **Practice Assertive Communication:** You can be assertive without being aggressive. Rehearse how you will say "no" in front of a mirror or with a trusted friend to learn this vital skill.

✅ **Respond with Emotional Intelligence:** When you practice self-compassion by saying "no," your ability to care for others increases as well.

REFLECTION

- If you were in Susan's place, would you have said "yes" to Cynthia?
- How can you practice small acts of saying "no" in daily life?

PROGRESS TRACKER: USING THE SUCCESS MODEL

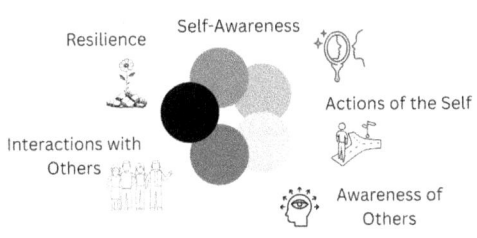

THE SUCCESS MODEL of EMOTIONAL INTELLIGENCE

Self-Awareness

✅ Realizes her tendency to help others at the expense of her own needs

Actions of the Self

✅ Understands that self-care is necessary for handling her stress and for relating to others in a healthy manner

✅ Begins to understand that caring for others means caring for herself, too

CHAPTER 13
JAKE

Jake is brilliant, bold, and barely house-trained when it comes to professional behavior. As a summer intern in a high-stakes law firm, he's got ideas to spare—but not much patience, polish, or tact. Can raw talent survive without Emotional Intelligence? Watch Jake learn (sometimes the hard way) that brains alone don't cut it.

Jake

JAKE'S SCENARIOS

- Not-So-Humble Beginning
- Blind Spots
- Is Perception Everything?
- Handling Hot Buttons
- Lying Awake
- Relax for Resilience

CHAPTER 14
NOT-SO-HUMBLE-BEGINNING

> *Make sure you're very courageous; be strong, be extremely kind, and above all be humble.*
>
> SERENA WILLIAMS

SCENARIO

Jake, a new intern in the Legal department of a large corporation, is listening in on a meeting of the Executive Team and Legal department as they discuss a possible government audit.

CEO: Before we adjourn, I'd like to give our new intern an opportunity to weigh in on the discussion. What questions or comments might you have about the direction we're heading in, Mr. McCarthy?

Jake leans forward in his chair, fully ready and eager to give his opinion.

Jake: This might surprise you, but I think you're headed in the wrong direction. I see at least two serious risks if you continue with your current assumptions.

The room goes silent. Jake, unfazed, confidently ticks off his points.

Executive: (*slamming his fist on the desk*) He's right! Why didn't Legal warn us about this? Have we been kept in the dark?

Tension rises. Voices clash. The meeting spirals until the CEO regains control.

CEO: Thank you, Mr. McCarthy. You've given us something to think about. We'll reconvene on Tuesday.

WHAT WOULD YOU THINK?

When we're certain we're right—or eager to prove our value—it's tempting to blurt out our views. However, others may also hold strong perspectives. Consider:

Emotionally Reactive Thoughts:

I've proven my worth already! They'll see I'm ahead of the game.

Reframe with Emotionally Intelligent Thoughts:

This isn't the reaction I wanted. Even if I'm right, I'm a newcomer, and others may see things differently.

JAKE'S NEXT STEP

We can choose our thoughts to guide our actions. See what you think of Jake's choice:

―――

I may be smart, I may be right, but… next time, I'd frame my insights as a question to invite dialogue instead of confrontation. Today's meeting was a wake-up call for me.

COACHING TIPS

Joining a team and becoming a trusted and respected member takes more than brilliant ideas.

✅ **Acknowledge the Work of Others:** Take time to get to know the strengths and expertise of team members. After presenting, ask for feedback on your delivery.

✅ **Leave Room for Humility:** Listening is not passive—it's how trust begins.

✅ **Respond with Emotional Intelligence:** Presenting ideas effectively builds respect and collaboration.

REFLECTION

- How can embracing humility turn your smart ideas into innovation?

PROGRESS TRACKER: USING THE SUCCESS MODEL

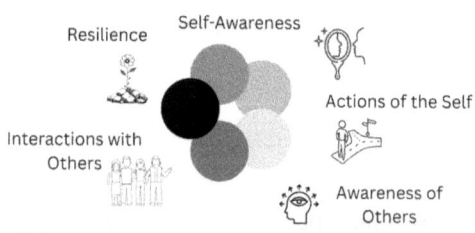

THE SUCCESS MODEL of EMOTIONAL INTELLIGENCE

Self-Awareness

☑ Becomes aware that his confident style is perceived as confrontational

Actions of the Self

☑ Intends to present ideas as questions to invite dialogue

Awareness of Others

☑ Recognizes the value of differing perspectives and has earned respect

Interaction with Others

☑ Begins to understand how humility earns trust and increases influence

CHAPTER 15
BLIND SPOTS

> At best, people are open to scrutinizing themselves and considering their blind spots; at worst, they become defensive and angry.
>
> SHERYL SANDBERG

SCENARIO

Jake checks in with mentor Michael Knowles to reflect on his first two months as an intern.

Jake (internal): *How did I get this guy? Well-respected, sure, but not the sharpest . . . is that a Ph.D. in computer science?*

Michael (mentor): Jake, I'd like to start with you. What have you learned so far?

Jake: I've learned a lot about Legal coordination with the exec team and about how it keeps the company out of trouble.

Michael: I've heard you're a smart problem solver. Are you feeling challenged enough?

Jake: Honestly, I've done well. But I don't exactly feel accepted.

Michael: I'm glad you brought that up, and we can talk more about it, but I suggest an Emotional Intelligence assessment and possibly some coaching. EQ is just as critical as IQ.

WHAT WOULD YOU THINK?

Even gentle suggestions can sting. Being told we're missing something takes self-awareness. Consider:

Emotionally Reactive Thoughts:

Are you kidding me? An emotional assessment? Total waste of time.

Reframe with Emotionally Intelligent Thoughts:

This guy is smart, respected, and maybe onto something. If he sees something I don't, I should pay attention.

JAKE'S NEXT STEP

We can choose our thoughts to guide our actions. See what you think of Jake's choice:

This could be my proverbial "blind spot." An assessment—and possibly a coach—might be helpful. Vulnerable? Yes. But necessary.

COACHING TIPS

☑ **Seek Honest Feedback:** Use assessments or ask a trusted colleague.

✅ **Consider Feedback, Even if it Stings:** Acknowledging blind spots opens the door to personal growth.

✅ **Respond with Emotional Intelligence:** Don't dwell—adjust and move forward.

REFLECTION

- How would you respond to feedback about a blind spot?
- How can you learn about possible blind spots?

PROGRESS TRACKER: USING THE SUCCESS MODEL

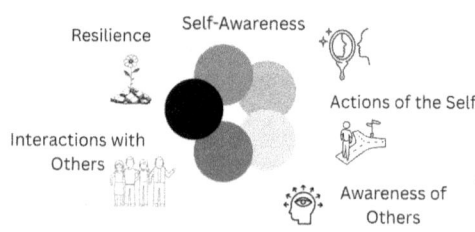

THE SUCCESS MODEL of EMOTIONAL INTELLIGENCE

Self-Awareness

✅ Realizes that fitting in takes more than intelligence

✅ Becomes aware of how others perceive him

✅ Considers that EQ may be just as important as IQ for success

Actions of the Self

✅ Accepts his mentor's feedback and plans to take an EI assessment

CHAPTER 16
IS PERCEPTION EVERYTHING?

> *Our perceptions of others are our realities about them. This is the law of perception.*
>
> MICHELLE TILLIS LEDERMAN

SCENARIO

Jake and another intern, Leigh, participate in a meeting regarding a liability strategy. Jake observes as Leigh presents her opinion.

Leigh: Both sides have made valid points. Maybe a different approach could help. Are you open to that?

Nodding of heads around the table. She continues.

Jake (internal): *Smiling? Asking permission? That's not me. But everyone listens to her. Leigh is brilliant, but not smarter than me! What's her secret?*

Executive: Thank you, Leigh. Jake—your thoughts?

WHAT WOULD YOU THINK?

It's tough to admit someone else's style works better. But observing successful communicators can be a shortcut to EI growth. Consider:

Emotionally Reactive Thoughts:

I could solve this in two seconds. I'm not going to bow and smile.

Reframe with Emotionally Intelligent Thoughts:

Leigh gets results. Perhaps I can learn from how she engages others.

JAKE'S NEXT STEP

We can choose our thoughts to guide our actions. See what you think of Jake's choice:

I've read that how you say something may be as important as what you say. I'm going to study Leigh's approach—and others who connect well in meetings.

COACHING TIPS

If you become more aware of how you are being perceived, you can adjust your words and actions to communicate more effectively for better outcomes.

✅ **Increase Awareness of Your Audience:** Pay attention to body language and energy in the room.

✅ **Learn from a Role Model Who is an Effective Communicator:** Ask a skilled colleague how they'd phrase something.

✅ **Respond with Emotional Intelligence:** Adjust your tone to create clarity and connection.

REFLECTION

- What's one thing you could do to make your communication more audience-centered?

PROGRESS TRACKER: USING THE SUCCESS MODEL

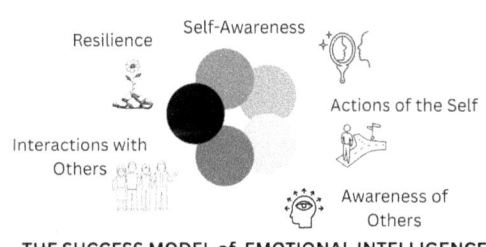

THE SUCCESS MODEL of EMOTIONAL INTELLIGENCE

Self-Awareness

✅ Realizes how tone and delivery shape perceptions

Actions of the Self

✅ Decides to study communicators who earn respect

Interaction with Others

✅ Begins adapting style to increase clarity and connection

CHAPTER 17
HANDLING HOT BUTTONS

> *The most fundamental harm we can do to ourselves is to remain ignorant by not having the courage and the respect to look at ourselves honestly and gently.*
>
> PEMA CHODRON

SCENARIO

Jake calls his coach in frustration after being passed over for a major assignment in favor of Leigh.

Coach: Your voice message sounded urgent, Jake. What's going on?

Jake: Leigh got the case! They know how smart I am!

Coach: What other criteria, besides intelligence, do you think they based their decision on?

Jake: (*mumbles*): How should I know?

Coach: Can you tell me how you're feeling right now?

Jake: (*loudly*) I'm damn angry!

Coach: Anything else?

Jake: (*pause*) I'm—disappointed, I guess. Maybe a little jealous.

Coach: Good. Naming emotions is the first step to managing them.

Jake: Is this where you tell me to breathe?

WHAT WOULD YOU THINK?

Strong emotions are normal, but they can be managed. Learning how to name and navigate them builds resilience. Consider:

Emotionally Reactive Thoughts:

I'm too smart to be falling for this woo-woo stuff. Emotions are for therapy junkies. I don't need to talk about feelings.

Reframe with Emotional Intelligence:

Okay, I don't like this, but my coach might be onto something. If I can manage my emotions, I can make better choices—and maybe even change the outcome next time.

JAKE'S NEXT STEP

We can choose our thoughts to guide our actions. See what you think of Jake's choice:

———

If I can manage my emotions, I can figure out why I was passed over—and make the necessary adjustments. I'm going to start naming how I feel in the moment!

———

COACHING TIPS

Recognizing and managing your emotions is a skill that can be learned — but not overnight. This skill takes practice over time.

✅ **Name Your Emotions:** Don't just feel—label it. Angry? Disappointed? Jealous?

✅ **Understand the Amygdala Hijack:** Fight or flight reactions can hijack clarity. Take a pause.

✅ **Respond with Emotional Intelligence:** All emotions provide useful information. Use your feelings as valid data—not destructive drama.

REFLECTION

- What emotions do you recognize in yourself during a tough moment?

PROGRESS TRACKER: USING THE SUCCESS MODEL

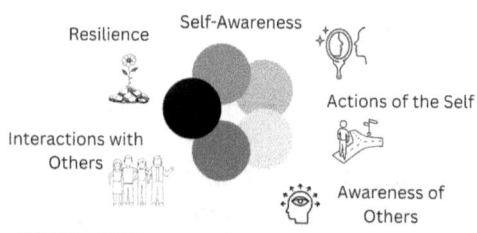

THE SUCCESS MODEL of EMOTIONAL INTELLIGENCE

Self-Awareness

☑ Learns to identify emotions beyond anger, like jealousy and disappointment

Actions of the Self

☑ Starts labeling emotions to manage them more effectively

Resilience

☑ Discovers how emotional awareness improves responses and recovery.

CHAPTER 18
LYING AWAKE

It takes much more than just hearing to listen intentionally, mindfully, and thoughtfully.

DEBORAH L. WALKER

SCENARIO

It is 3:30 am, and Jake has been tossing and turning, haunted by a fight with Jill.

Jake: *I can't lose her, she's the best thing that ever happened to me. She said I don't listen. Don't respect her. That makes me sound terrible.*

Jake's inner voice: *Is she the only one who sees you like that? What about people at work? What would they say about you?*

Jake: *My coach warned me. Leigh says that sometimes I miss what people are saying when I think I already know.*

Jake's inner voice: *She might be right.*

Jake: *How do I fix this? How do I really listen?*

WHAT WOULD YOU THINK?

Honest self-talk reveals what feedback sometimes can't: the need for real change. Consider:

Emotionally Reactive Thoughts:

Okay, so I don't have a PhD in listening. But why does everyone act like it's some superpower?

Reframe with Emotionally Intelligent Thoughts:

My habits are hurting my relationships. It's time to learn what real listening means.

JAKE'S NEXT STEP

We can choose our thoughts to guide our actions. See what you think of Jake's choice:

The coach mentioned "active listening"—not waiting to talk but truly hearing someone. I need to learn that.

COACHING TIPS

There's more to listening than allowing sounds to enter your ears.

☑ **Set the Intention to Listen:** Act like you'll have to summarize the speaker's key points.

☑ **Observe and Offer Cues.** Body language, facial expression, and voice speak volumes–and so do yours.

☑ **Respond with Emotional Intelligence**. Acknowledge feelings. Learn from what's shared.

REFLECTION

- Who do you know who listens well? What effect do they have on you?

PROGRESS TRACKER: USING THE SUCCESS MODEL

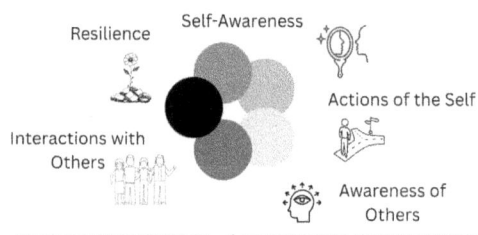

THE SUCCESS MODEL of EMOTIONAL INTELLIGENCE

Self-Awareness

☑ Acknowledges his poor listening and its consequences

Actions of the Self

☑ Uses self-talk to process and plan improvement

Awareness of Others

☑ Understands others feel disrespected when not truly heard

Interaction with Others

☑ Commits to building better relationships through listening

CHAPTER 19
RELAX FOR RESILIENCE

The time to relax is when you don't have time for it.

SYDNEY J. HARRIS

SCENARIO

Jake and his girlfriend Jill sit on a log next to a campfire near their tent. The night is incredible, and they stare up at the multitude of stars above them.

Jill: Dinner was excellent. I had no idea you were an expert outdoor chef!

Jake: I listened to what you told me would please you, but I had no idea how much I'd enjoy it. Thank you for this—being out here in such a beautiful place.

Jill: I am impressed, but much more than by your gourmet grilling. I'm impressed with the change I've seen in you during these last few weeks. You actually hear what I'm saying. It makes such a difference in our relationship. I'm grateful, Jake.

Jake: Yeah. Active listening. Slowing down. Working on both, thanks to you. Thank you for urging me to take breaks instead of working all the time. I can't tell you what a change that has made for me.

Jill: Look at all those stars. I'm seeing a fantastic future for us.

WHAT WOULD YOU THINK?

Letting go of old habits opens space for new ones that enrich our well-being. Consider:

Emotionally Reactive Thoughts:

What if I haven't really changed? Coach said this would take a lot of practice. Can I keep this up?

Reframe with Emotionally Intelligent Thoughts:

This is working. Listening with intention is changing everything, for the better.

JAKE'S NEXT STEP

We can choose our thoughts to guide our actions. See what you think of Jack's choice:

———

I'm sticking with this! Active listening is a key component in building trust—at work and with Jill.

———

COACHING TIPS

☑ **Be Open to Change:** Acknowledging a weakness is a strength.

☑ **Practice and Observe:** Try the new skill in different settings. Track the results.

☑ **Respond with Emotional Intelligence:** Practice leads to stronger connections—and a clearer mind.

REFLECTION

- What small change in how you interact could transform your relationships?

JAKE'S PROGRESS TRACKER

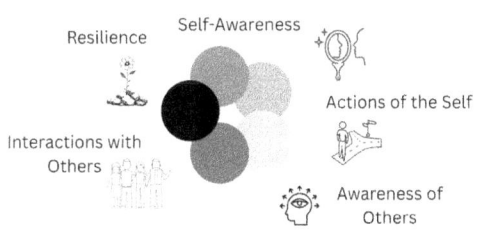

THE SUCCESS MODEL of EMOTIONAL INTELLIGENCE

Awareness of Others

☑ Intentionally practices listening to understand

Interaction with Others

☑ Sees how listening deepens the relationship

Resilience

☑ Learns that stepping back to recharge improves effectiveness and balance

CHAPTER 20
MARJORIE

Precise, polished, and utterly in control, Marjorie runs a high-end department store floor like a military operation. But life has a way of softening sharp edges. As pressures mount and emotions crack through, Marjorie begins to discover that efficiency isn't everything, and kindness might just be her superpower.

MARJORIE'S SCENARIOS

- You Be the Judge?
- The Five-Minute Reset
- Beyond Policy
- Competition or Collaboration
- The Unseen Struggle
- Joy and Suffering

CHAPTER 21
YOU BE THE JUDGE?

When you judge another, you do not define them; you define yourself.

WAYNE DYER

SCENARIO

Marjorie is observing her sales team on a busy afternoon. She has her eye on a recent hire (a niece of the store manager), Kiki, a young woman with a ring in her nose and two more in her eyebrow.

Marjorie (internal): Kiki won't last here long. You can tell just by looking at her that she doesn't belong here. And how she manages running around in those ridiculous pink platform shoes all day is beyond me!

Marjorie's thoughts are interrupted by a commotion in the women's shoe section. A middle-aged woman has fainted and is lying on the floor next to a pile of shoeboxes.

Marjorie (internal): *Oh no, I don't need another problem today. If she's injured, the store may be liable. I'd better call security to take care of this.*

Meanwhile, Kiki makes her way through the gathering crowd. She bends down and finds a Medical Alert bracelet on the woman's wrist.

Kiki: (*putting her arm under the woman's head*) "She's diabetic!"

She looks around and points to an onlooker who has a plastic beverage container in her hand.

Kiki: Is that a cola--regular, not diet? Can I have it for this woman--it's an emergency!

Marjorie: No, wait--I'll call 911. We can't treat her ourselves, it's not our responsibility, and it could be a liability to the store

Kiki: (*ignoring Marjorie*) She's regaining consciousness.

Marjorie: But... what if...

Kiki: (*speaking to the woman*) Ma'am, you seem to have fainted. How are you feeling now? Do you carry any glucose tabs--or can you drink a few sips of this cola?

Woman who fainted: Yes, in my purse, in a silver pill box--thank you . . .

WHAT WOULD YOU THINK?

It is often difficult for us to admit that we were wrong. We rely on internal biases, some of which we may not even be aware of, to judge other people. Even when proven wrong, we often want to hold on to those initial thoughts. Consider the following possibilities:

Emotionally Reactive Thoughts:

Kiki ignored me--just defied my authority! And in front of all these people. Just took over as if she were the one in charge! I won't stand for this. I knew she was bad news.

Reframe with Emotionally Intelligent Thoughts:

I have learned something important from Kiki, who I was so wrong about. Her empathy as well as her quick thinking were critical in this situation.

MARJORIE'S NEXT STEP

We can choose our thoughts to guide our actions. See what you think of Marjorie's choice:

―――

How did I let myself fall into stereotyping this young woman solely based on her appearance? I know better than that! Turns out she has a lot to teach me about managing my emotions in a crisis.

―――

COACHING TIPS

The old saying, "Don't judge a book by its cover," is even more meaningful when applied to people.

☑ **Hold Back Judgement:** Don't let fear, ignorance, or bias lead you to misjudge someone different from you, whether that is appearance, ethnicity, gender, political or religious leanings, or level of education.

☑ **Evaluate on Objective Data:** Give people time, and one way or another, they will show what they are made of.

☑ **Respond with Emotional Intelligence:** Focus on a person's potential growth and the possibility of building a relationship. Remain curious!

REFLECTION:

- If you were in Marjorie's place, how would you have reacted to Kiki's appearance?

PROGRESS TRACKER: USING THE SUCCESS MODEL

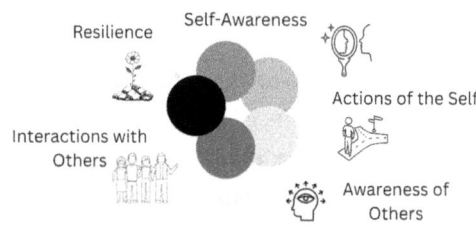

THE SUCCESS MODEL of EMOTIONAL INTELLIGENCE

Self-Awareness

☑ Recognizes she misjudged an employee based on her appearance and ego-driven assumptions

Awareness of Others

☑ Acknowledges her lack of empathy in a crisis

Interaction with Others

☑ Begins shifting focus from liability concerns to supporting people in real time

CHAPTER 22
THE FIVE-MINUTE RESET

> *Almost everything will work again if you unplug it for a few minutes-- including you.*
>
> ANNE LAMOTT

SCENARIO

Marjorie sits alone in her office computing a rough estimate of shoe sales for the quarter. She is feeling anxious and stressed.

Marjorie: *To remain at the top, our department must do more. Gary's dragging the team down--should I cut him loose? I've got to visit Dad tonight--hope he gets out of the hospital soon. And the schedule? Still a mess.*

Marjorie's inner voice: *You're exhausted--admit it. You're over-committed. A spa weekend would be lovely, but no, no time for that now.*

Marjorie: *Nothing is going right. That special order didn't arrive today. Nancy called in sick. Two of my salespeople seem to be at war* with each other. I hope Dad is okay. Should I let Gary go? What if . . . And the cat needs to see the vet.

Marjorie's inner voice: *Whoa! Your thoughts are becoming increasingly negative and repetitive. What did that coach say about that? Your blood pressure is rocketing upwards.*

Marjorie: *The coach said to take a five-minute "worry break" at a scheduled time. And something about having a more positive mindset.*

WHAT WOULD YOU THINK?

The chatter that goes on in our minds continually can be harnessed to produce honest self-reflection, which can lead to positive outcomes. Consider:

Emotionally Reactive Thoughts:

A worry break--really? As if I have time for that! And I'm not Pollyanna--I can't make negative situations into positive ones. None of that is helpful.

Reframe with Emotionally Intelligent Thoughts:

I could try one of the coach's techniques for lessening stress and anxiety. Let's see . . . there was the breathing technique, and the taking a walk outdoors idea, and listening to music diversion, exercise, of course, and meditation ...

MARJORIE'S NEXT STEP

We can choose our thoughts to guide our actions. See what you think of Marjorie's choice:

> *I've got it! The coach said to start small, taking baby steps. I will put aside all these issues and take a five-minute pause—a worry break—today at 4:00!*

COACHING TIPS

Negative thinking, worry, over-scheduling, and a driven style can all take a toll on your mental health.

☑ **Notice Your Negativity:** Recognize how often you think or say something negative--in your self-talk, with friends and family, or with colleagues.

☑ **Give Yourself a Break:** Interrupt the cycle of negative thoughts by declaring a designated time to worry. A five-minute break can transform your workday.

☑ **Respond with Emotional Intelligence:** Find your anxiety-reliever--whether that is deep breathing, yoga, exercise, music, poetry, hiking, gardening, knitting, or some other activity that is meaningful to you.

REFLECTION

- What helps you to cope with anxiety and stress?

PROGRESS TRACKER: USING THE SUCCESS MODEL

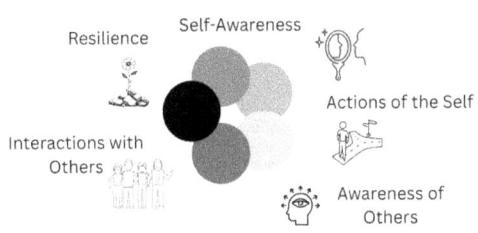

THE SUCCESS MODEL of EMOTIONAL INTELLIGENCE

Self-Awareness

☑ Notices repetitive negative thoughts and the toll of exhaustion and stress

Actions of the Self

☑ Recalls coaching strategies and takes one small, intentional step: scheduling a worry break

CHAPTER 23
BEYOND POLICY

> *The highest form of knowledge is empathy, for it requires us to suspend our egos and live in another's world.*
>
> PLATO

SCENARIO

Marjorie, manager of the shoe department, is called to handle a disgruntled customer.

Marjorie (internal): *Deep breath. Stay open. Listen first.*

Mrs. R (customer): Your salesman has been incredibly rude! I've tried to explain--these shoes are unacceptable. I got blisters the first time I wore them!

Josh (salesman): Ma'am, I've explained the store's policy. We offer refunds within three months. You bought them over six months ago and don't have . . .

Mrs. R: (*raising her voice*): I told you--I was away! This policy. Is absurd!

Marjorie takes in the woman's tense posture, her shaking hands. She catches herself before reacting out of frustration. Instead of judging, she wonders: What's going on here?

Marjorie: (*calmly*) I'm so sorry this has been frustrating, Mrs. R. Let's see what we can do.

Instead of pushing back, Marjorie softens. Not long ago, she would have shut this down fast.

Marjorie: It sounds like you've had a rough time. Would you mind telling me what's been going on?

Mrs. R: (*in tears*)I was overseas taking care of my sister. She passed away. And now--this. I just--I don't know why everything has to be so hard."

Marjorie nods. *There it is.*

Marjorie: I'm so sorry for your loss. Let's take care of this for you.

She motions for Mrs. R. to follow her to the counter.

Josh: (*muttering*) But... the policy--

Marjorie turns to him, speaking quietly but firmly.

Marjorie: "People matter more than policies."

WHAT WOULD YOU THINK?

Anyone who manages people would recognize the constant need to balance organizational regulations and concerns with the need to meet the needs of other people, whether employees or customers. Consider:

Emotionally Reactive Thoughts:

Another entitled customer making a scene. This is manipulation. I'd rather call security than deal with this.

Reframe with Emotionally Intelligent Thoughts:

Something is wrong beyond the shoes. Perhaps she's struggling financially, or perhaps she's just overwhelmed. Either way, I can choose to be kind.

MARJORIE'S NEXT STEP

We can choose our thoughts to guide our actions. See what you think of Marjorie's choice:

"We want you to be satisfied with your purchase, Mrs. R. Let's make this right."

COACHING TIPS

In an emotionally charged confrontation, it may be not easy to empathize, but it's a skill you can develop.

☑ **See Beyond the Outburst:** People often express frustration when they're struggling with something else. Ask yourself what else might be happening in this person's life.

☑ **Empathize.** Imagine for a moment that this person is someone you know and love--a family member or a close friend. How would you want to see them treated?

☑ **Respond with Emotional Intelligence:** Listen first, validate feelings, and find a reasonable solution.

REFLECTION

- If it is in your power to be kind, why not be kind?

PROGRESS TRACKER: USING THE SUCCESS MODEL

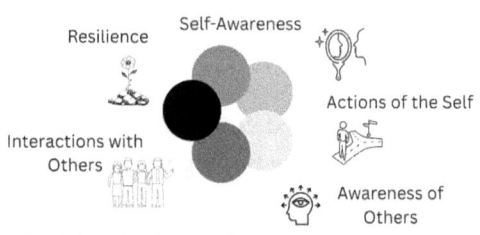

THE SUCCESS MODEL of EMOTIONAL INTELLIGENCE

Awareness of Others

☑ Sees past a customer's anger to recognize emotional distress

Interaction with Others

☑ Listens without judgment, shows empathy, and chooses compassion over rigid policy

CHAPTER 24
COMPETITION OR COLLABORATION

Coming together is a beginning, staying together is progress, and working together is success.

HENRY FORD

SCENARIO

arjorie calls salesmen Dennis and Joseph into her office. Their rivalry has fueled department tension, and last week, it nearly turned physical.

Marjorie: You two are our top sellers. I appreciate your drive. But lately, that competition has made the rest of the team uneasy.

Dennis: They don't try. Selling takes hustle.

Joseph: They don't read customers like I do.

Marjorie (internal): *They don't respect the team. No wonder morale is sinking.*

Marjorie: I get it. You're both at the top for a reason. But let me ask — what would it take to increase total sales by 15% over the next six months?

Dennis: How? I'm already maxed out.

Joseph *(grinning)*: Yeah, and I'm beating him. If you're expecting me to hand over my techniques, think again.

WHAT WOULD YOU THINK?

As a leader, it may sometimes seem easier to blame others rather than take the responsibility to lead them. Consider:

Emotionally Reactive Thoughts:

They're selfish and don't care about teamwork. Maybe I need to fire one — or both. Who needs this constant rivalry?

Reframe with Emotionally Intelligent Thoughts:

My job as a leader is to build a team. If only I could redirect their competitive energy somehow.

MARJORIE'S NEXT STEP

We can choose our thoughts to guide our actions. See what you think of Marjorie's choice:

———

"I need you two to take the lead on something big. A new high-end brand is launching, and we need experts. If we do this right, we all win. Can I count on you?"

———

COACHING TIPS

A leader may need to think creatively to inspire a sense of collaboration rather than competition among team members.

✅ **Assess the Culture:** Competition can be healthy, but if it undermines morale, it's a problem.

✅ **Get Creative:** Turn rivalry into motivation for the whole team.

✅ **Respond with Emotional Intelligence:** People unite around common goals--whether in sports, disaster relief, or business. Tap into that energy.

REFLECTION

- What inspires you to work as part of a team?

PROGRESS TRACKER: USING THE SUCCESS MODEL

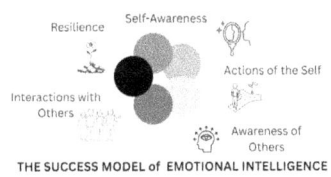

THE SUCCESS MODEL of EMOTIONAL INTELLIGENCE

Self-Awareness

✅ Accepts her role in shaping a healthy team dynamic

Awareness of Others

✅ Recognizes both strengths and blind spots in her top performers

Interaction with Others

- ☑ Channels competitive energy into a team-building opportunity

CHAPTER 25
THE UNSEEN STRUGGLE

Empathy is seeing with the eyes of another, listening with the ears of another, and feeling with the heart of another.

ALFRED ADLER

SCENARIO

Marjorie sighs as she glances at the monthly sales report on her desk. A young saleswoman, Yvonne, sits across from her.

Marjorie: I gave you a month to turn things around, Yvonne. Your sales have not improved…

Yvonne: No, ma'am.

Marjorie: It's not fair to expect the rest of the team to make up for your lack of effort.

Yvonne is silent, biting her lip. Then she begins speaking with a rush of words.

Yvonne: It's—it's not a lack of effort, ma'am. Truly. Please, I need this job.

Marjorie (internal): *Oh no, here it comes. I'm the villain who has the power to crush or save you. Do you think I like making decisions like this?*

Marjorie: Look, I'm not made of iron, Yvonne. I can see from looking at you that something's wrong. Do you want to tell me what's going on with you?

Again, Yvonne hesitates but then pours out her story. She's not going to like listening to my excuses.

Yvonne: My ex is out of work and drinking every day. My mother has been ill. And my two-year-old is facing serious ear surgery. I have nowhere to turn . . .

WHAT WOULD YOU THINK?

Staying open to listening to another's story is a gift -- listening opens the door for greater empathy. It provides more information for weighing actions and words to decide as a manager. Consider:

Emotionally Reactive Thoughts:

I hate this part of my job—listening to stories like this. It puts a lot of pressure on me to do something. People don't understand that my responsibilities as a manager give me little choice.

Reframe with Emotionally Intelligent Thoughts:

Yvonne has always been a reliable employee, if not a top producer. But no wonder her sales have fallen! She is overwhelmed with worry for her family. I can't do much to help, but I can empathize and try to make things a little easier.

MARJORIE'S NEXT STEP

We can choose our thoughts to guide our actions. See what you think of Marjorie's choice:

"Thank you for sharing your situation, Yvonne. This must be a challenging time for you, and I'm so sorry. Here are a couple of things I can do to help. I'm going to connect you with our company's Employment Assistance Fund, and I can make your schedule lighter during the next few weeks."

COACHING TIPS

☑ **Ask and Listen:** People may be shy or embarrassed about a personal situation. Reach out gently to indicate that you are willing to listen.

☑ **Empathize:** Be prepared as you listen to put yourself in the other person's place to understand what is happening and to acknowledge their pain. Practice compassion even when performance falters—there may be more going on than you know.

☑ **Respond with Emotional Intelligence:** Find a human connection beyond the constraints of business concerns.

REFLECTION

- What is a leader's responsibility for the personal lives of employees?

PROGRESS TRACKER: USING THE SUCCESS MODEL

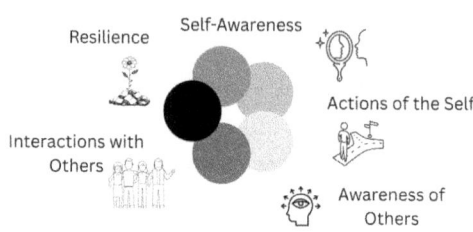

THE SUCCESS MODEL of EMOTIONAL INTELLIGENCE

Self-Awareness

☑ Realizes her leadership position may make her seem cold or inflexible

Actions of the Self

☑ Opens the door for honest conversation with a struggling employee

Awareness of Others

☑ Responds with empathy and practical support based on personal understanding

Interaction with Others

☑ Acts with compassion to reduce pressure and connect on a human level

CHAPTER 26
JOY AND SUFFERING

> *Everything can be taken from a man but one thing: the last of the human freedoms--to choose one's attitude in any given set of circumstances, to choose one's own way.*
>
> VIKTOR E. FRANKL

SCENARIO

Marjorie sits beside her father's hospital bed as a nurse adjusts his pillows, helping him sit up for her visit.

Dad: *(smiling weakly)* Marji, you brighten my world.

Marjorie: *(squeezing his hand)* I should be here more often. Work is swallowing me whole. And Marcos is frustrated--I barely see him. How am I supposed to juggle everything? Maybe I need to clone myself.

Dad: Nonsense. The world only needs one Marjorie.

Marjorie: *(lowering her gaze)* I shouldn't be complaining. Not when you're here--like this.

Dad: Ah, but that's life: suffering and joy, both. And I am grateful for all of it.

Marjorie blinks back tears, studying his frail face. *How does he do it?*

Marjorie: *(whispering)* Dad, how do you always stay so calm?

He takes her hand in both of his, his grip lighter than she remembers.

Dad: It's no secret. I have seen suffering--in my own life and in the lives of people throughout history. But Viktor Frankl said it best: no matter what, we get to choose our attitude.

Nurse: I'm sorry, but your dad needs to rest now.

Marjorie nods, pressing his hand before letting go. She walks out feeling lighter, his words lingering.

WHAT WOULD YOU THINK?

Sometimes, we gain a new perspective when we weren't even looking. Consider:

Emotionally Reactive Thoughts:

I can't stand seeing him like this. It's too painful. And the guilt--why don't I make more time for him? My life is too overwhelming. . .

Reframe with Emotionally Intelligent Thoughts:

This is Dad's wisdom in action. Life will always have challenges. But if he can embrace joy and suffering with grace, so can I.

MARJORIE'S NEXT STEP

We can choose our thoughts to guide our actions. See what you think of Marjorie's choice:

> Life is short. Dad has shared with me the wisdom of his years—that life is suffering and joy. I have the choice to focus on challenges--or on what truly matters. Thanks, Dad.

COACHING TIPS

We don't need to be on our deathbed to realize the preciousness of life and our inherent ability to choose how to respond to life's ups and downs.

☑ **Pause and Reflect:** Take a mental step back and notice the stories you tell yourself about your life and responsibilities. What if you changed those stories to include gratitude and joy?

☑ **Train Your Mind:** Whether through meditation, prayer, or mindfulness--cultivate the ability to align your actions with your core values.

☑ **Respond with Emotional Intelligence:** Self-awareness and resilience help us accept both suffering and joy with grace.

REFLECTION

- How have your experiences, culture, and relationships shaped your perspective on life?

PROGRESS TRACKER: USING THE SUCCESS MODEL

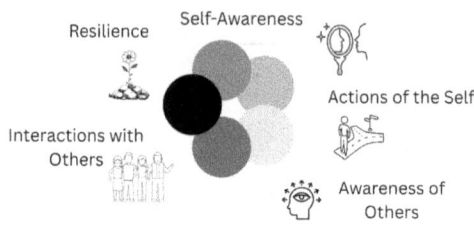

THE SUCCESS MODEL of EMOTIONAL INTELLIGENCE

Self-Awareness

✅ Recognizes the self-defeating stories she tells herself about being overwhelmed

Actions of the Self

✅ Seeks her father's perspective and absorbs his calm wisdom

Resilience

✅ Begins choosing to face life's difficulties with grace and focus on what matters most

CHAPTER 27
ANTHONY

Anthony's always been the smartest guy in the room—just ask him. But as his executive team pushes back and his personal life frays at the edges, even he starts to question if maybe being right isn't always enough.

ANTHONY'S SCENARIOS

- Lone-Wolf CEO
- Taking the Blame
- Overusing Strengths
- Pivot with Self-Talk
- Behind Closed Doors
- Nature's Power

ANTHONY

CHAPTER 28
LONE-WOLF CEO

> *No matter how brilliant your mind or strategy, if you're playing a solo game, you'll always lose out to a team.*
>
> REID HOFFMAN

SCENARIO

Anthony kicks off his exec meeting with a bombshell--he's finalized a merger.

Silence.

Dawn (exec team member): Sir, why were we left out of this decision? We are your executive team.

Anthony: Actually, Jim and Eduardo knew about this last week, and they're fully on board. Mergers are delicate. I couldn't risk leaks.

Dawn (internal): *He doesn't trust us! After all my years here?*

Seth (exec team member): We understand, sir, but shouldn't we have had some say? This will affect all of us.

Mark (exec team member): What do we even know about this other company? Are we replaceable? I have two kids in college.

WHAT WOULD YOU THINK?

A team's unfavorable response to a leader's decision can come as a surprise. Whether it is warranted or not, it deserves careful consideration. Consider:

Emotionally Reactive Thoughts:

What's with all this pushback? They should be celebrating my genius!

Emotionally Intelligent Thoughts:

I miscalculated. My team feels shut out. Trust is slipping--and that isn't good for business. And relationships.

ANTHONY'S NEXT STEP

We can choose our thoughts to guide our actions. See what you think of Anthony's choice:

This isn't the reaction I expected! I'm used to calling the shots alone, but I may have ignored valuable input. I need the team to make it work. I guess I made a mistake in not including them.

COACHING TIPS

The fastest route to decision-making, the unilateral decision, may result in a lack of trust and decreased motivation among team members.

✅ **Speed Kills Trust:** A fast, unilateral decision might save time, but it loses buy-in. Don't rush a decision so fast that you trample on the people who have to execute it.

✅ **Build the Bridge Before Crossing It:** A decision is only one step. Gaining support is just as critical.

✅ **Respond with Emotional Intelligence:** Consider input before locking in significant change.

REFLECTION

- How does a leader's decision-making style impact team motivation and trust?

PROGRESS TRACKER: USING THE SUCCESS MODEL

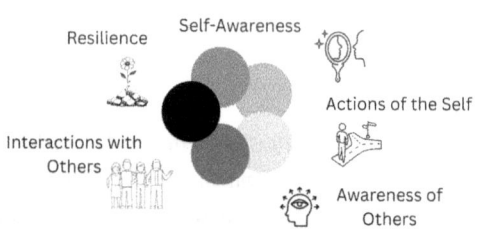

THE SUCCESS MODEL of EMOTIONAL INTELLIGENCE

Self-Awareness

✅ Becomes aware of others' perceptions of him when they push back with their questions

✅ Surprised by the team's resistance, he reflects on how his leadership style may alienate others

Awareness of Others

☑ Realizes that excluding team input erodes trust and reduces buy-in, even when decisions are well-intentioned

☑ Becomes aware that leadership is not just about making decisions—it's about bringing people along

CHAPTER 29
TAKING THE BLAME

A good leader is a person who takes a little more than their share of the blame and a little less than their share of the credit.

ARNOLD H. GLASGOW

SCENARIO

Anthony is meeting with his executive team on a Monday morning.

Anthony: Let's begin with a status report on our new project. Alicia, I believe you have the latest federal regulations?

Alicia: Uh--no, I don't believe I was assigned to obtain those, but…

Anthony: *(impatiently)* We can't move forward on this project without that information! Do you realize this could mean that we don't meet the filing deadline?

Alicia is clearly embarrassed and stammers as she answers the CEO.

Alicia: I… I can get to work on that immediately, but…

Harry enters the meeting room--he is late. Everyone is silent.

Harry: Sorry, I'm late. I needed to make copies of the new regulations so we could all look at them. I think you'll find them interesting.

WHAT WOULD YOU THINK?

Strong decision-making does not include snap judgments, impatience, or a defensive attitude. Consider:

Emotionally Reactive Thoughts:

This is going to make me look like a bully--again. Why do I always end up in these situations? It's not like I was wrong--Harry was late!

Emotionally Intelligent Thoughts:

Uh-oh. Looks like my impatience has trapped me this time. Alicia is being polite, but she does not deserve my anger. How do I admit my mistake?

ANTHONY'S NEXT STEP

We can choose our thoughts to guide our actions. See what you think of Anthony's choice:

———

"Alicia, no wonder you were hesitant. I'm sorry I jumped to conclusions--and it's my turn to be embarrassed. You, on the other hand, receive credit for being kind and diplomatic. Thank you."

———

COACHING TIPS

When we've failed at something or made a mistake, we tend to want to blame someone or something else. Our attempts to "save face," however, can backfire.

☑ **Acknowledge the Error:** Pause and breathe. Don't try to hide or downplay the mistake--especially if someone else is involved.

☑ **Accept Blame:** Be as ready to accept blame when you have made an error as you would be prepared to take credit when all goes well.

☑ **Respond with Emotional Intelligence:** In accepting responsibility, a leader creates greater trust in their team and becomes a more effective leader.

If you were in Anthony's place, how would you have handled this error? How does taking responsibility for mistakes or failures affect the team and the organization?

PROGRESS TRACKER: USING THE SUCCESS MODEL

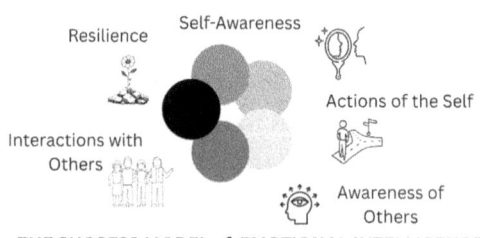

THE SUCCESS MODEL of EMOTIONAL INTELLIGENCE

Self-Awareness

☑ Acknowledges his error in publicly (and wrongly) blaming an employee

Actions of the Self

☑ Models emotional maturity by owning the mistake and restoring team confidence

☑ Learning that accountability can strengthen leadership and team trust

CHAPTER 30
OVERUSING STRENGTHS

> *Our greatest strengths, when taken to extremes, can become our greatest liabilities.*
>
> — UNKNOWN

SCENARIO

After a meeting in which Anthony angrily dismissed a suggestion to postpone development of a product in the company's pipeline, one of the executives shows up at his office to tender her resignation.

Joan (VP of production): You're not going to want to hear this, Anthony, but I'm giving you notice and submitting a letter of resignation.

Anthony: Joan? I don't understand. You're my right-hand man-- er, woman! (smiles) Here, please sit down and talk to me.

Anthony (internal): *What is happening and why? I never expected this. I need Joan on this team.*

Joan smiles wryly but sighs and sits in a chair opposite Anthony's desk.

Anthony: Wait, is this because I rejected your idea to postpone the product development? I didn't mean to--

Joan: Look. The Board brought you here, Anthony, because of your reputation for brilliant ideas and vision--which I can and do admire. However, your reluctance to work collaboratively with the team is something I find unacceptable.

WHAT WOULD YOU THINK?

Collaboration isn't a matter of style—it's a necessity for developing a creative, productive, and successful team. Consider:

Emotionally Reactive Thoughts:

She can't do this to me! I have a clear vision for this company, and I know how to move to action. She wants to slow me down.

Emotionally Intelligent Thoughts:

I've been blindsided by my desire to make quick, independent decisions and act on them. I need to reverse this situation. Indeed, I'm not great at collaboration. How can I change this style to work more effectively with my team?

ANTHONY'S NEXT STEP

We can choose our thoughts to guide our actions. See what you think of Anthony's choice:

———

"I owe you an apology, Joan--I am truly sorry. Despite what my behavior today would seem to indicate, I very much respect your ideas, and I need you on this team. Please withdraw your resignation--I'm asking you to reconsider staying on. And I will make every effort to

listen more and consider the ideas from you and the entire team."

COACHING TIPS

Sometimes it takes the shock of a "wake-up call" (like Anthony experienced when a valued employee resigned) to bring about real internal change.

✅ **Dampen Your Ego:** Don't be blind to the fact that an overuse of your strengths can lead to problems, especially in your interactions and relationships with others.

✅ **Check Your Past Experiences:** Be honest with yourself. Is this the first time someone has pointed out this flaw in your management style?

✅ **Respond with Emotional Intelligence:** Make amends, if possible, with a sincere apology followed by actions that demonstrate your efforts to change.

REFLECTION

- If you were in Anthony's place, how would you have reacted to Joan's resignation?
- What strengths do you have that you might be overusing?

PROGRESS TRACKER: USING THE SUCCESS MODEL

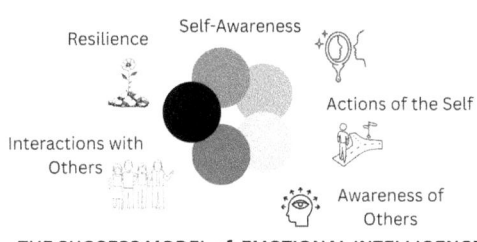

THE SUCCESS MODEL of EMOTIONAL INTELLIGENCE

Self-Awareness

☑ Begins to realize how others perceive him

☑ Realizes his action-oriented strength has limited his ability to engage others effectively

Actions of the Self

☑ Accepts direct feedback about his style and begins rethinking how decisions are made

Awareness of Others

☑ Becomes aware of how his lack of collaboration affects a key employee

CHAPTER 31
PIVOT WITH SELF-TALK

It's not what you say out of your mouth that determines your life; it's what you whisper to yourself that has the most power!

ROBERT T. KIYOSAKI

SCENARIO

Anthony is driving to work on a Los Angeles freeway at 7:30 am. He is listening to a podcast on self-talk that his coach suggested.

Anthony: *Huh! I always thought talking to yourself was a sign of being nuts! My teenagers are already doing a good job of driving me crazy!*

Anthony's inner voice: *The guy on the podcast said you don't have to talk out loud to do self-talk. Just try it--in your head.*

Anthony: *Okay. Let's take this morning as an example. That argument with my teenagers about weekend curfew drove my blood pressure up. I still haven't recovered!*

Anthony's inner voice: *Is that what you want to focus on now--the* kids--here in crazy traffic? What about that important meeting with the research division today?

Anthony: *Yeah. Important meeting. That guy Pierre always manages to piss me off. How will I deal with that?*

Anthony's inner voice: *You still have fifteen minutes before you get to work. Can you use it to prepare and forget about the kids for now?*

WHAT WOULD YOU THINK?

Taking time—ahead of time-- to rehearse your expected reactions to a conflict situation can help you manage your emotions when emotions heat up. Consider:

Emotionally Reactive Thoughts:

Sh…! That guy nearly cut me off! This day off to a bad start, and it's not even 8 am. My kids are mad at me, and I doubt this meeting will go well.

Emotionally Intelligent Thoughts:

Okay, I'm going to focus. When Pierre makes one of his complaints or delivers a criticism, I'm not going to go bananas as usual. I need to review those steps for managing my frustration.

ANTHONY'S NEXT STEPS

We can choose our thoughts to guide our actions. See what you think of Anthony's choice:

―――

> *I'm going to listen, pause, and respond calmly, no matter who says what, just like my coach recommends. I can do this!*

―――

COACHING TIPS

When you know you'll be facing a difficult situation, especially one in which emotions will be running high, it's worth taking some time to prepare.

✅ **Predict:** Imagine various scenarios for an upcoming interaction (whether with an individual or a roomful of people). See yourself in that situation. (Example: The division manager will be loudly critical of my decision.)

✅ **Prepare:** Use self-talk to determine 1) how you want to feel after the meeting and 2) what objectives you want to achieve. (Example: I want to feel that I've remained calm and professional and that we agree on the next steps for this project.)

✅ **Respond with Emotional Intelligence:** Self-talk can help you pivot to a more positive state by reframing negative thoughts. Explore both your fears and hopes as you make predictions and preparations for various situations.

REFLECTION

- Is self-talk always positive?
- What can you do if negative thoughts appear during your self-talk?

PROGRESS TRACKER: USING THE SUCCESS MODEL

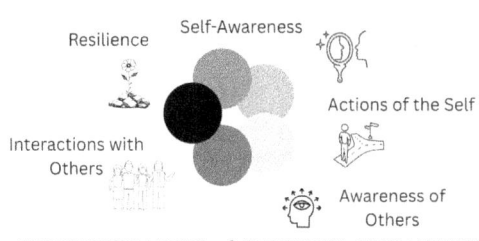

THE SUCCESS MODEL of EMOTIONAL INTELLIGENCE

Self-Awareness

☑ Realizes his tendency to react negatively to criticism and complaints

☑ Notices how his mental habits shape his mood and reactions, especially in stressful moments

Actions of the Self

☑ Learning how to prepare himself with self-talk to take a more positive attitude when facing a difficult situation

☑ Uses self-talk to pause automatic reactions and rehearse a more intentional response

CHAPTER 32
BEHIND CLOSED DOORS

Criticism is something we can avoid easily by saying nothing, doing nothing, and being nothing.

ATTRIBUTED TO ARISTOTLE

SCENARIO

After a lengthy phone call, Anthony stretches his legs in the hallway. He pauses outside the employee break room when he hears laughter--his name has just been mentioned.

Stan (employee): It's a good idea, but I wouldn't try talking to him today. I heard he was in one of his foul moods over the merger.

Millie (employee): But when I mentioned my idea to him last week, he seemed interested. It's a great way to help people and boost our reputation.

Rick (employee): Go ahead if you want to, but don't expect a thank-you. That's not in the boss's DNA!

Laughter.

Anthony stiffens and turns back to his office, shaken.

WHAT DO YOU THINK?

Criticism can sometimes punch us in the face! It takes self-awareness and an attitude of humility to face criticism. Consider:

Emotionally Reactive Thoughts:

How dare they? I hold this place together. Moody? If they had my job, they'd be moody too.

Emotionally Intelligent Thoughts:

Criticism is a gift--who said that? I feel blindsided and yeah, it stings. But if this is how they see me, I need to take it seriously. I don't want to be the boss nobody thanks.

ANTHONY'S NEXT STEP

We can choose our thoughts to guide our actions. See what you think of Anthony's choice:

―――――

Two weeks later, an email was sent to all company staff: You're invited to a casual lunch this Friday from noon to 2:00. Les Crêpes will take your custom order — savory or sweet. I appreciate all your hard work this quarter. Hope to see you there! --Anthony Sepe, CEO

―――――

COACHING TIPS

Understanding how others perceive us takes self-awareness.

✅ **Pause Your Defense:** Whether overhearing gossip or receiving formal feedback, resist the urge to dismiss it.

✅ **Look for Patterns:** Not every comment matters, but repeated themes deserve attention. Where can you improve?

✅ **Respond with Emotional Intelligence:** Plan a small, concrete step to address the criticism.

REFLECTION

- If you overheard something similar about yourself, how would you react?

PROGRESS TRACKER: USING THE SUCCESS MODEL

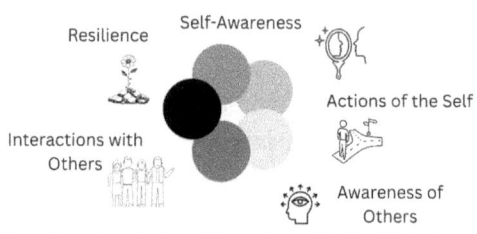

THE SUCCESS MODEL of EMOTIONAL INTELLIGENCE

Self-Awareness

✅ Becomes aware of how others perceive him

Awareness of Others

☑ Realizes that others will have reactions to what he says and does

Actions of the Self

☑ Takes criticism seriously despite being shocked to hear it

☑ Takes visible steps to express appreciation and improve team morale

CHAPTER 33
NATURE'S POWER

Nature's peace will flow into you as sunshine flows into trees. The winds will blow their own freshness into you, and the storms their energy, while cares will drop off like autumn leaves.

JOHN MUIR

SCENARIO

Anthony's old friend Frank drags him on a day hike in the national park. It's beautiful, but the trail is steep.

Anthony (internal): *This reminds me of college days. I miss this. But a whole day away? I have a huge meeting on Monday.*

Frank: You seem stressed, Tony. Everything okay?

Anthony: You know--teenagers at home, work's a beast. And I'm feeling my age! How much farther?

Frank: Hear that? The falls! Lunch spot ahead.

They reach the overlook--water cascades into a valley bathed in sunlight. Anthony exhales.

WHAT WOULD YOU THINK?

Sometimes, something unexpected in the natural world—listening to bird song in a quiet forest, viewing a spectacular sunrise, observing the peak flowering of a cherry tree in springtime—can deeply and mysteriously affect us. Consider:

Emotionally Reactive Thoughts:

What a waste of time. I should be prepping, not sweating up a mountain.

Emotionally Intelligent Thoughts:

This view. This stillness. Stress feels . . . distant. I need more of this.

ANTHONY'S NEXT STEP

We can choose our thoughts to guide our actions. See what you think of Anthony's choice:

———

I've rediscovered the power of nature to change my perspective. I had forgotten that for too long. Note to self: get outside and enjoy my life and this beautiful world.

———

COACHING TIPS

Self-care fosters resilience, which can lead to a healthier and longer life.

✅ **Self-Care Isn't Selfish:** Eating well, sleeping enough, music, friends, and nature all fuel resilience and the strength to face the inevitable challenges of life.

✅ **Mindfulness Isn't Woo-Woo:** It's a skill. Learning to let go of what you can't control brings peace.

✅ **Respond with Emotional Intelligence:** Build resilience by reconnecting with what restores you.

REFLECTION

- What's one simple way you could reconnect with the natural world this week?

PROGRESS TRACKER: USING THE SUCCESS MODEL

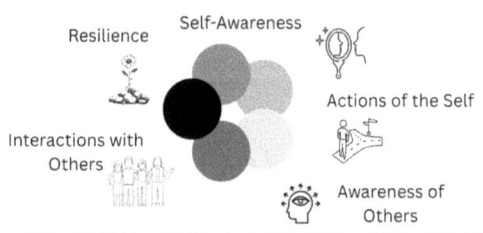

THE SUCCESS MODEL of EMOTIONAL INTELLIGENCE

Self-Awareness

✅ Becomes aware of something he has lost or ignored over many years

✅ Acknowledges the internal transformation from feeling stressed to feeling relaxed and renewed by being outdoors

Actions of the Self

✅ Recognizes the value of stepping away to reset and recharge emotionally

Resilience

☑ Begins to build resilience by integrating restorative experiences into his life

CHAPTER 34
EMILY

Emily's energy lights up every room—until it doesn't. Driven, passionate, and deeply caring, she's also prone to second-guessing and emotional overwhelm. As she learns to steady herself in the storm, Emily discovers that Emotional Intelligence isn't about dialing things down—it's about tuning in with intention.

EMILY'S SCENARIOS

- Words and Intent Matter
- The Email Meltdown
- Winning People Over
- Get Curious
- Playing to Your Strengths
- Effective Emails

CHAPTER 35
WORDS AND INTENT MATTER

> *It is well to remember that the entire population of the universe, with one exception, is composed of others.*
>
> ANDREW J. HOLMES

SCENARIO

Emily starts her Monday with a structured routine: a morning walk, a quick breakfast, and an early arrival at the office. She organizes materials for the CEO and begins jotting notes.

Just as she's deep in thought, Sidney, a new hire, appears at her desk.

Sidney: I have a meeting in five minutes and just realized I need budget estimates for the new program. Can you help me?

Emily briefly turns to look at Sidney.

Emily: I think that was emailed last week—it should be in your inbox.

She returns to her computer.

Sidney sighs and walks away, looking frustrated.

WHAT WOULD YOU THINK?

Even in brief interactions, our intentions are communicated not only by our words but also by our tone of voice, facial expressions, and body language. Consider:

Emotionally Reactive Thoughts:

Not my problem. He needs to be more organized.

Reframe with Emotionally Intelligent Thoughts:

Sidney looked stressed. And he's new here. Did I come across as dismissive?

EMILY'S NEXT STEP

We can choose our thoughts to guide our actions. See what you think of Emily's choice:

"Morning, Sidney. You need those figures? Let me grab the link for you. Just so you know, for next time, they're in the end-of-the-month report."

COACHING TIPS

Our intent matters in every interaction and is reflected in our words, in our tone of voice, and in our body language. How aware are you of your intentions when you interact?

✅ **Pause:** What was Emily's intent when she responded—to inform, dismiss, or help Sidney? By taking the time to consider the impact your response will have on both the other person and yourself, you gain a valuable perspective.

✅ **Empathize:** Intentions are reflected in tone, body language, and facial expressions, even if quite subtle. How did Sidney feel in this scenario? Frustrated? Embarrassed? Angry?

✅ **Respond with Emotional Intelligence:** Acknowledging requests while maintaining boundaries builds better dynamics and strengthens relationships.

REFLECTION

- How would Sidney have felt if Emily had offered a more supportive response in the first place?
- How would Emily have felt responding differently?

PROGRESS TRACKER: USING THE SUCCESS MODEL

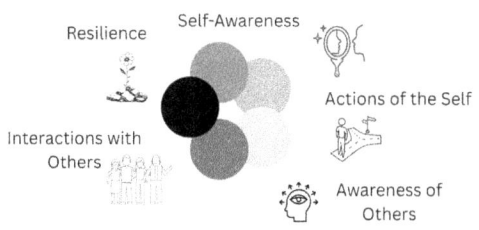

THE SUCCESS MODEL of EMOTIONAL INTELLIGENCE

Self-Awareness

☑ Begins to realize that her intent and words have an impact in any interaction

Awareness of Others

☑ Recognizes her assumptions and chooses to seek clarity before overreacting defensively

Interactions with Others

☑ Carefully chooses her words and tone to be supportive, thus fostering collaboration rather than tension

CHAPTER 36
THE EMAIL MELTDOWN

To err is human--and to blame it on a computer is even more so.

ROBERT ORBEN

SCENARIO

mily's hands are shaking as she ties the laces on her sneakers at lunchtime. She is desperate to get outside, away from the office.

The morning had started with an interruption in the organization's communications system. Incoming emails could not be replied to, and new emails could not be sent. As the CEO's admin, she had become the hub for angry complaints and demands.

Outside, she takes a deep breath and looks up at the sky. Snow is threatening, but she knows that taking a walk may help. It was the one thing she knew would help her feel calm again.

A few minutes later, large wet flakes of snow began swirling around her. Emily stands still and tips her head back to feel the cool flakes on her face.

She is filled with a sense of the beauty of nature and her small part in it all, something she was aware of when she was snowboarding or hiking, but rarely has an opportunity to slow down and enjoy otherwise.

She turns to walk back to the office and faces the disgruntled employees.

WHAT WOULD YOU THINK?

Coping with stress in the workplace requires self-awareness and the ability to take a broader perspective. Consider:

Emotionally Reactive Thoughts:

This is ridiculous! I'm the punching bag for every tech issue. Do I look like an IT Wizard? Maybe I should wear a cape. My head is about to explode. How do I solve everyone's problems?

Reframe with Emotionally Intelligent Thoughts:

What's that old line? Don't sweat the small stuff--and it's all small stuff? Why didn't I realize this before? A problem with email is that it's small stuff, and anyway, I can't fix it!

EMILY'S NEXT STEP

We can choose our thoughts to guide our actions. See what you think of Emily's choice:

Why didn't I see this before? I'm not responsible for either the issue or the emotions of the complainers. It's totally out of my control. That's a relief!

COACHING TIPS

Sometimes our "hot buttons" get pushed, and we're off! Furious, hurt, or disappointed. And in that state, we're not ready to let go of how we feel.

☑ **Pause:** As always, the first step to managing an emotion is to acknowledge and identify it. Our emotions are complex, and accurately labeling them can be helpful. Are you feeling frustrated? Overwhelmed? Under-appreciated?

☑ **Search for Perspective:** How important is this problem/issue? How important will it be in a day? In a week? In a month? What consequences might it have for me, my family, or my colleagues?

☑ **Respond with Emotional Intelligence:** Once you've taken time to view the problem from a broader perspective, can you let it go? If not, can you try to find a calm response that will lead to a healthy way of managing (not "controlling") how you feel?

REFLECTION

- Have you ever been wrongly blamed for something? Or, like Emily, did you have to take the heat for issues you didn't cause?
- When emotions run high, taking a pause isn't about ignoring how you feel--it's about choosing how you respond. What would it take for you to let go and move forward?

PROGRESS TRACKER: USING THE SUCCESS MODEL

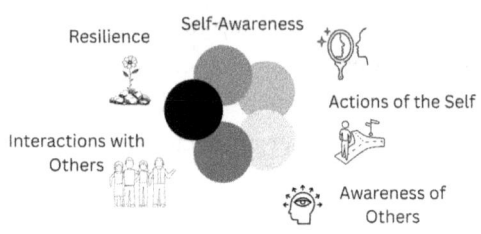

THE SUCCESS MODEL of EMOTIONAL INTELLIGENCE

Self-Awareness

☑ Recognizes that she has taken on stress that is not her responsibility

☑ Recognizes the need for self-regulation before re-entering a high-stress situation

Actions of the Self

☑ Realizes that some things are out of her control

☑ Lets go of trying to fix the situation or manage the emotions of others

CHAPTER 37
WINNING PEOPLE OVER

We have two ears and one tongue so that we would listen more and talk less.

DIOGENES OF SINOPE

SCENARIO

mily and Johanna, her best friend at work, are sitting on high stools at a new tapas bar, enjoying wine and a baked brie appetizer after work on a Friday afternoon.

Johanna: This feels civilized and comforting! Thanks for suggesting this place. So, my friend, what did you want to ask me about?

Emily: I'm so excited about introducing this new management software to the staff. How do you think my presentation went at this morning's meeting?

Johanna: Em, you're my dear friend, so I want to be honest with you. I think the software is promising and much needed. It doesn't look difficult to train everyone on. You convinced me.

Emily: But . . .?

Johanna: May I offer you some advice based on my own experience?

Emily: Of course.

Johanna: Your presentation was right on--almost intimidating. *(smiles)* However, I've learned that people need to be heard — complaints, concerns, questions, whatever. You anticipated objections, but you didn't provide time to listen to their reactions.

WHAT WOULD YOU THINK?

Feedback can be offered harshly or humanely. It can be received with hostility or humility. Consider:

Emotionally Reactive Thoughts:

Listen? To what--complaints? People love to resist change. I made everything crystal clear, but some people don't want to move forward. Why waste my time coddling them?

Reframe with Emotionally Intelligent Thoughts:

Wow. I've always admired Johanna's ability to connect with people, and I think I just saw why she's so effective. It's not just about presenting information--it's about making people feel heard. I completely missed that step.

EMILY'S NEXT STEP

We can choose our thoughts to guide our actions. See what you think of Emily's choice?

"I worked so hard to make that presentation perfect, but

you've made me realize that I skipped one of the most important aspects--listening to people. Thank you, Johanna."

———

COACHING TIPS

It can be challenging to ask for feedback or advice. And even more difficult to absorb and act on it. But feedback, even when it seems negative or poorly delivered, is almost always a gift.

✅ **Hit the Brakes on Your Ego:** You may feel a need to defend yourself, but take a breath.

✅ **Be Willing to Try it Out:** Even tough feedback usually has some truth in it. Don't dismiss it outright. Take time to consider whether it applies to you.

✅ **Respond with Emotional Intelligence:** No matter what the feedback, you don't need to argue against it or defend yourself, but commit to exploring whether the input can be helpful to you.

REFLECTION

- If you were in Emily's shoes, how would you respond to Johanna's feedback?

- Feedback isn't always easy to hear, but it's often the key to growth. The next time you receive feedback, will you dismiss it--or will you listen for the insight that could make you better?

PROGRESS TRACKER: USING THE SUCCESS MODEL

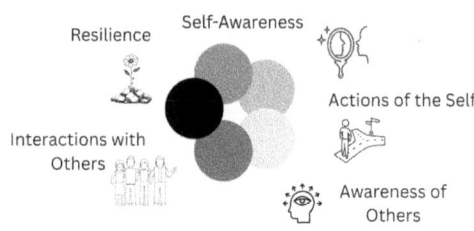

THE SUCCESS MODEL of EMOTIONAL INTELLIGENCE

Actions of the Self

☑ Pauses to consider feedback from a coworker/mentor whom she trusts

☑ Identifies a valuable EI strength in a colleague and chooses to emulate it

Awareness of Others

☑ Realizes that people need more than information—they need to feel heard

CHAPTER 38
GET CURIOUS

Replace judgment with curiosity.

LYNN NOTTAGE

SCENARIO

The CEO turns to Emily, his admin, who is taking notes at a board meeting.

Ted Wilson, CEO: I would like to recognize Emily, who has taken on the significant task of coordinating and editing all the sections of the annual report as they are submitted by staff. Ready to go to press on Friday, Emily?

Looking up from her laptop, Emily feels her face growing red.

Emily: Almost there!

Emily (internal): *But I still haven't heard from Janice. If she doesn't get it to me soon, she's going to make me look incompetent. I've sent reminder after reminder. She's putting me in an impossible spot.*

After the meeting, Emily knocked on Janice's office door. She is angry.

Janice: Hi, Emily. Listen, I'm so sorry, I know that . . .

Emily: Janice! You look… frazzled. Are you okay?

Janice: Well, actually, no.

Janice bursts into tears and grabs a tissue in embarrassment.

WHAT WOULD YOU THINK?

When we feel threatened in some way, our defenses kick in to protect our ego, and we may then find it difficult to empathize. Consider:

Emotionally Reactive Thoughts:

This is such unprofessional behavior. Crying in the office! I'm not falling for it. I need that information to do my job, and I'm going to let her know that!

Reframe with Emotionally Intelligent Thoughts:

Wow, this is not like Janice. Something must be very much the matter. Maybe I can help.

EMILY'S NEXT STEP

We can choose our thoughts to guide our actions. See what you think of Emily's choice:

> "Janice, I've never seen you so upset! I'm so sorry. Would you like to talk about it? Perhaps we can figure something out together."

COACHING TIPS

Sometimes we live so much within our own bubble that we fail to understand what others are thinking and feeling.

✅ **Pause and Ask:** What assumptions am I making about the person or their behavior? What if my assumptions are wrong?

✅ **Be Curious:** Could there be another explanation for this person's behavior? Use your imagination to step out of your bubble and into the other person's bubble for a few moments. What is it like in there?

✅ **Respond with Emotional Intelligence:** Assumptions can shape your stories and actions. Pausing to "get curious" can turn conflict into connection. Could you please share your story about this person and adopt a more empathetic approach?

REFLECTION

- What if you were in Emily's shoes? Would you confront Janice?
- How might you rewrite your story about Janice?

PROGRESS TRACKER: USING THE SUCCESS MODEL

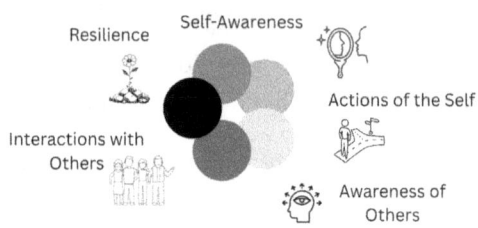

THE SUCCESS MODEL of EMOTIONAL INTELLIGENCE

Awareness of Others

☑ Becomes aware of her tendency to blame rather than seeking to understand

☑ Learning to question the story she tells herself about a colleague's behavior

Actions of the Self

☑ Expands her perspective to include the feelings of others, not just her own distress

☑ Replaces blame with empathetic inquiry

CHAPTER 39
PLAYING TO YOUR STRENGTHS

Play to your strengths. They're your greatest assets.

WENDY NICOLE ANDERSON

SCENARIO

It's a sunny Saturday morning. Amos and Emily are training their Jack Russell Terriers on an obstacle course at the park. Amos stands on the sidelines with a stopwatch.

Amos: Go, Harold! Go Maud! Go Emily!

They take a break at a nearby picnic table, the dogs resting at their feet.

Emily: Maud is so good at agility, but Harold is fearless and fast through the tunnels. I think they both enjoy it, and they're really improving.

Amos pours a cup of coffee for Emily from a thermos. She sips in silence, frowning slightly.

Amos: You look lost in thought, Em. What's going on in that beautiful mind of yours?

Emily: Oh, I was thinking about the character strengths survey that I took at work last week. I didn't score very high on humor, bravery, teamwork, and a few others. I feel like these are areas where I should improve.

Amos: Hmm. Perhaps you're missing the point, my love. Isn't the survey meant to identify your character strengths? Why focus on your lowest scores? What about your top scores-- honesty, perseverance, and sound judgment?

WHAT WOULD YOU THINK?

While recognizing flaws is helpful for self-development, understanding and leveraging your unique strengths can lead to positive outcomes. Consider:

Emotionally Reactive Thoughts:

I hate these surveys. Now everyone at work will think I'm dull, timid, and uncooperative. Maybe I should force myself to laugh more, say things I'm not sure of, and try harder to fit in.

Reframe with Emotionally Intelligent Thoughts:

Amos may be right. He sees my strengths clearly, yet I've been so focused on my perceived weaknesses that I've overlooked what I bring to the table. I need to start valuing myself the way he does.

EMILY'S NEXT STEP

We can choose our thoughts to guide our actions. See what you think of Emily's choice:

> "I'm going to write my strengths on a Post-it and stick it on my computer to remind me to use them more often."

COACHING TIPS

Several surveys, like the one Emily took, are available online. Even without a survey, take time to reflect on both your strengths and areas for growth.

☑ **Identify Your Strengths:** Are you a great listener? A creative problem-solver? Someone who makes people feel at ease? Strengths come in many forms — acknowledge yours.

☑ **Consciously Employ Your Strengths:** Once you've identified and appreciated your strengths, make it a point to consciously use them more every day, to "play to your strengths."

☑ **Respond with Emotional Intelligence:** By focusing on your strengths, on what you do best, you can build your confidence and be yourself.

REFLECTION

- If you were in Emily's place, would the lower scores on the survey of strengths bother you? Why?
- What unique strengths do you bring to your workplace that others might appreciate more than you realize?

PROGRESS TRACKER: USING THE SUCCESS MODEL

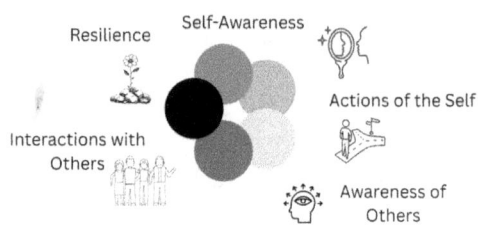

THE SUCCESS MODEL of EMOTIONAL INTELLIGENCE

Self-Awareness

☑ Learning to focus more on her unique strengths rather than her weaker points

Actions of the Self

☑ Takes action to give herself reminders of an idea she has realized as important to her

☑ Consciously decides to build her confidence by focusing on what she brings to the team

CHAPTER 40
EFFECTIVE EMAILS

I wish 'you dumbass' was an appropriate way to end a work email.

QUIRKY CARD COMPANY

SCENARIO

Emily opened an email from the organization's Chief Financial Officer, George Mattson.

Dear Ms. Evans: I'm putting you on notice. If you ever embarrass me again as you did in today's strategic planning meeting, you will no longer be working here. I remind you that I oversee all budget matters in this organization. Your position as an admin, even as admin to the CEO, does not entitle you to make unsolicited suggestions regarding budget or spending cuts without consulting with me first.

Emily took a deep breath. She was sure she could feel adrenaline or cortisol or whatever the heck it was pouring into her bloodstream to nudge her to "fight or flight."

She quickly typed out a reply to Mr. Mattson:

Dear Mr. Mattson,

Thank you for your kind email. I want to remind you that you are a dinosaur as well as a bully. Everyone knows that, and you should be ashamed of yourself for accusing and insulting me when you don't even have all the facts. My suggestion was the result of considerable discussion with my boss and a committee formed to investigate and recommend a replacement schedule for computers and printers company-wide. I believe you were informed of our work and received our written recommendations. You just couldn't stand it that a woman, a mere admin assistant, could speak up in a meeting to make a suggestion. Everyone knows that you want to take credit for everything, even if you have nothing to do with it! I, for one, will no longer stand for your bullying. I'm looking forward to your retirement in January!

Emily left the email in her drafts folder, brewed a cup of chai tea, and focused on completing her morning's work.

WHAT WOULD YOU THINK?

It's possible to hold contrasting thoughts at the same time. Fortunately, we can learn to manage our emotions and make constructive choices. Consider:

Emotionally Reactive Thoughts:

Part of me would still like to send this draft email to old Mr. Mattson., He's so behind the times, and it's time for him to retire. He's not going to bully me just because he's the CFO and I'm a lowly admin. I want to hit him with a nasty email!

Reframe with Emotionally Intelligent Thoughts:

Now that I've cooled down, I have to chuckle at how strongly I reacted. Why is that? If I were to send that original email, I would be disrespecting the man, not his position, but his humanity, a person with his own needs and fears. I can find some compassion for him when I'm not feeling angry. Not to mention that to send that nasty email would be to shoot myself in the foot.

EMILY'S NEXT STEP

We can choose our thoughts to guide our actions. See what you think of Emily's choice:

———

Hours later, Emily opens her draft email, reads it, and laughs out loud. Then she revises:

Dear Mr. Mattson:

Thank you for your note regarding yesterday's strategic planning meeting. It was certainly not my intention to leave you out of the loop, and I'm sorry if it seemed so to you.

Would it be helpful if we sat down to review the committee minutes and recommendations? I'd be happy to schedule a time that works for you.

———

COACHING TIPS

Our first reactions are often the products of ancient structures in our brains that are meant to protect us from harm. We can learn to recognize that initial surge of energy, but soften it to formulate a response that will not make things worse.

✅ **Acknowledge the Feeling:** You may identify fury, hurt, or disappointment, for example. Name the feeling or feelings as specifically as you can.

✅ **Take a Break:** Find a way to remove yourself from the situation. Go for a walk. Grab a beverage or a snack. Stare at the clouds. Read a poem or a quote that reminds you of your values and intentions as a human being. Take a break to develop options that will result in more positive actions.

✅ **Respond with Emotional Intelligence:** When you've given yourself time to regain your composure, treat that first draft email like an incendiary device! Take the time necessary to disarm it before you push "send."

REFLECTION

- If you were in Emily's place, how would you respond to Mr. Mattson's email?

PROGRESS TRACKER: USING THE SUCCESS MODEL

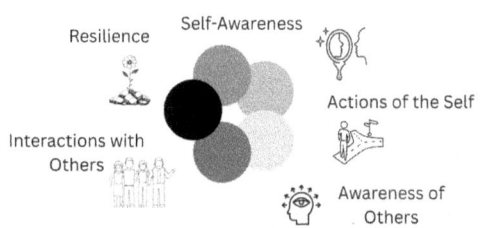

THE SUCCESS MODEL of EMOTIONAL INTELLIGENCE

Self-Awareness

✅ Recognizes that her initial reactions may not be beneficial

Actions of the Self

- ☑ Makes a conscious pause and returns to rewrite the email

Awareness of Others

- ☑ Practicing what she has learned previously to be more aware of others' emotions

CHAPTER 41
JUAN

Juan is a calm, capable college dean with a passion for students and a mile-long to-do list. He prides himself on keeping calm under pressure—but when people's problems heat up, he's forced to lean into emotions he usually keeps at arm's length. It turns out that quiet leaders can grow loud in all the best ways.

JUAN

JUAN'S SCENARIOS

- Gaining Support for Your Vision
- The Assumption Trap
- Why Didn't They Hear Me?
- Dismiss or Discover?
- Seeing with New Eyes
- The Power of Recognition

CHAPTER 42
GAINING SUPPORT FOR YOUR VISION

> *Too often, shared visions really mean, 'I have a vision; you share it!'*
>
> ANDY HARGREAVES

SCENARIO

Juan, dean of the IT program at a community college, has spent months crafting a proposal to expand the IT curriculum. He speaks with enthusiasm as he wraps up a presentation to faculty.

Juan: These AI animation courses will put our department and our college in a unique position. More importantly, they will create exciting career paths for our students! Any questions or comments?

Louis, a long-time faculty member of the college, doesn't hesitate to speak up angrily.

Louis: Yeah! I have questions! How do you propose we pay for course development and new instructors to teach "cartoon making"? What makes you think you know what our students want? I don't understand what you're doing! This proposal is unrealistic.

WHAT WOULD YOU THINK?

Criticism, especially when delivered in a public forum, can feel like a personal attack. Responding in the moment takes strong self-awareness as well as an awareness of others. Consider:

Emotionally Reactive Thoughts:

I'm doing my job, you idiot! Time to get rid of old guys like you who have no vision for the future. You're humiliating me in front of the faculty. Wait till you see my evaluation of your teaching!

Emotionally Intelligent Thoughts:

Whoa--this guy is angry. Louis has been here a long time and wants to keep the status quo. It looks like I have some work to do to earn his trust. I need everyone on board to make this successful.

JUAN'S NEXT STEP

We can choose our thoughts to guide our actions. See what you think of Juan's choice:

"You're right, Louis. This proposal has significant implications for budgeting and hiring. But that doesn't make it impossible. If you — and anyone else interested—are open to it, I'd love to share some of the data and trends related to AI. How about a lunchtime brown bag next week?"

COACHING TIPS

Listening and reacting to personal insults, perhaps especially in a public forum, can feel brutal. Learning how to respond in the moment may take some practice.

Hold Back the Daggers! Take a deep breath or two before responding. Stay calm and rational, and build trust with your audience.

Find Common Ground: Validate any part of the concern you can. Ask for input and show openness.

Respond with Emotional Intelligence: Public pushback is a leadership test. Your response sets the tone.

REFLECTION

How would you respond to Louis's questions and concerns in this public forum?

- How do you build trust in your workplace?

PROGRESS TRACKER: USING THE SUCCESS MODEL

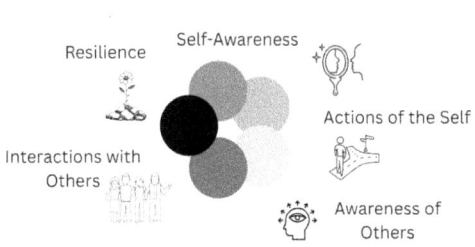

THE SUCCESS MODEL of EMOTIONAL INTELLIGENCE

Awareness of the Self

✅ Realizes trust must be earned

Actions of the Self

✅ Stays calm in the face of public criticism

Interaction with Others

✅ Acknowledges concern and invites collaboration

CHAPTER 43
THE ASSUMPTION TRAP

> *Your assumptions are your windows on the world. Scrub them off every once in a while or the light won't come in.*
>
> ALAN ALDA

SCENARIO

Juan is on a Zoom call with his leadership coach.

Coach: How are things going with the faculty member that you call the "old hippie" who was "resisting your authority?"

Juan: Wow, I really said that? *(laughs)* I'm not used to having my words reflected back to me. But I owe you.

Coach: You preferred to avoid him. Has that changed?

Juan: Yeah. Turns out I was utterly wrong about Kevin. I assumed that he was just riding out his tenure, but his students love him. He has some of the highest success rates in the department. And get this--he's an avid wildlife photographer, just like me.

WHAT WOULD YOU THINK?

We make assumptions about people within the first minute of meeting them. That doesn't mean that we are right. Consider:

Emotionally Reactive Thoughts:

When my coach first suggested that I take Kevin to lunch, I wanted to roll my eyes. I keep work and personal life separate. What do coaches know about difficult faculty?

Emotionally Intelligent Thoughts:

Wow, almost everything I assumed about Kevin was wrong. Now I actually admire him, and I'm learning from him.

JUAN'S NEXT STEP

We can choose our thoughts to guide our actions. See what you think of Juan's choice:

> "You've taught more students than I have. What was it like when you first started? What keeps you passionate about teaching?"

COACHING TIPS

We all make assumptions about the people we interact with-- probably within the first few minutes of meeting them. To work successfully with a team or build strong relationships, we have to rely on more than those initial "gut" feelings.

☑ **Get Curious:** People are more complex than our snap judgments.

☑ **Ask Sincere Questions:** Open-ended questions build trust and connection.

☑ **Respond with Emotional Intelligence:** Give people a blank slate. Let them surprise you.

REFLECTION

- Think of a time you misjudged someone. What changed your perspective?
- What questions could you ask to get to know colleagues better?

PROGRESS TRACKER: USING THE SUCCESS MODEL

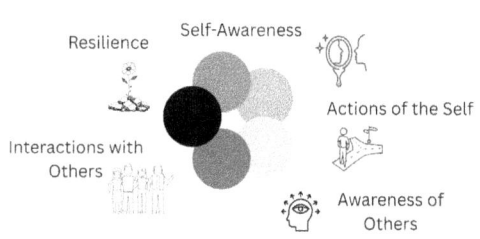

THE SUCCESS MODEL of EMOTIONAL INTELLIGENCE

Self-Awareness

☑ Realizes his tendency to judge a colleague with little or no knowledge of the person

☑ Articulates his mistakes and false assumptions

Interactions with Others

☑ Understands that the assumptions we make about people can be misleading

☑ Makes a conscious effort to build a relationship with a colleague

CHAPTER 44
WHY DIDN'T THEY HEAR ME?

I was still working at Google when I wrote the blog post '10 Tricks to Appear Smart in Meetings.' I was scared to share it at first because I didn't want my coworkers to think that I was making fun of them - which I totally was. But then afterward I had people coming up to me like, 'I have a meeting trick! Put my meeting trick in your next post!

SARAH COOPER

SCENARIO

The faculty of the college's IT program is discussing new curricula for the coming year.

Jasmine: If we create a survey for all incoming students who express interest in IT courses, we can gain useful statistics to back up our plan to offer advanced AI courses. As Ronda pointed out, we need to know both the level of knowledge and the interest of potential students.

Milton: Great idea, Jas! A survey like that is easy to set up, and it would also help us obtain development funding. I am aware of an industry grant for which we can apply.

Juan tightens his grip on his pen. *Didn't I just suggest the same idea ten minutes ago? Back then, it landed with a thud. Now, suddenly, it's brilliant?*

WHAT WOULD YOU THINK?

Contributing a valuable idea or opinion at a meeting requires more than intelligence. Consider:

Emotionally Reactive Thoughts:

Are you kidding me? I literally said this exact thing earlier, and no one even blinked. Now Jasmine says it, and she's a genius? This is ridiculous.

Emotionally Intelligent Thoughts:

That IS a good idea, and it was mine! But Jasmine managed to present it in a way that got buy-in. She's persuasive. Instead of stewing, I'm going to pay attention to how she does it.

JUAN'S NEXT STEP

We can choose our thoughts to guide our actions. See what you think of Juan's choice:

Jasmine seems to know how to get people on board. What's her secret? Is it her tone, timing, or something else? I'm going to observe her and find out.

COACHING TIPS

The solution to a problem or challenge may seem evident to us, but blurting out our brilliant idea may result in the idea falling flat or being ignored.

✅ **Know Your Audience:** Gauge the group's mood and interests before introducing your idea. Timing matters.

✅ **Listen and Build:** Reference others' points to create buy-in and help your ideas land.

✅ **Respond with Emotional Intelligence:** Observe skilled communicators and adapt their strategies.

REFLECTION

- Have you ever had your idea ignored at a meeting, only for someone else to repackage it and get the credit?
- What can you do to present your ideas more effectively?

PROGRESS TRACKER: USING THE SUCCESS MODEL

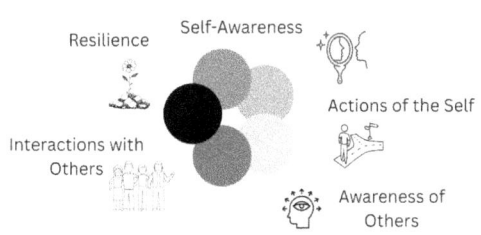

THE SUCCESS MODEL of EMOTIONAL INTELLIGENCE

Self-Awareness

- Becomes aware of how others perceive him

Actions of the Self

- Chooses to learn rather than react
- Observes and adapts communication techniques

CHAPTER 45
DISMISS OR DISCOVER

> *When we accept dismissive judgements of our community, we stop having generous hope for it. We cease to be capable of serving its best interests.*
>
> MARILYNNE ROBINSON

SCENARIO

Several students appear at Dean Juan Ramirez's office door.

Juan: Come in! If I had known a platoon was coming, I would have brought a shield and armor!

Jenine (student): Thank you, Dean Ramirez. We need to talk to you about Professor Murphy.

Juan: Let me guess--strict grading? Too much homework? High standards? Complaints should go to your instructor.

James (student): We've tried, sir.

Constance (student): It's like talking to a brick wall. For example, he has zero flexibility with attendance policies.

Juan: *(leaning back)*: Look, professors set their own policies. My hands are tied.

Alison (student): Dean Ramirez, respectfully--I've read your bio. You probably lived on campus and had family support. Most of us are working adults with jobs, families, and real-life struggles. If we get penalized for occasional tardiness, we are doomed from the start.

WHAT WOULD YOU THINK?

A leader is responsible for the people they serve. Strong leadership includes understanding and empathizing with their perspective. Consider:

Emotionally Reactive Thoughts:

Do I look like a complaint department? Your professor has rules--deal with it. If you can't handle it, maybe you don't belong here.

Emotionally Intelligent Thoughts:

I never thought about it from their perspective. I assumed their college experience was like mine, but that's not true at all.

JUAN'S NEXT STEP

We can choose our thoughts to guide our actions. See what you think of Juan's choice:

"That's a fair point! I'll talk with your professor. What other challenges are students facing that I should know about?"

COACHING TIPS

We don't like to hear criticism, and our first impulse may be to dismiss it, especially if it comes from an unexpected source. Our minds search for a way to either ignore the issue or put it off on someone else.

☑ **Listen for Who's Struggling:** Even if you're not responsible for hardship, acknowledging it shows respect.

☑ **Acknowledge Emotions:** You don't have to agree to show that you care.

☑ **Respond with Emotional Intelligence:** Step into someone else's world. Empathy is a bridge to better solutions.

REFLECTION

If you were in Juan's position, how would you have handled this?

- How do dismissive attitudes affect workplace or classroom culture?

PROGRESS TRACKER: USING THE SUCCESS MODEL

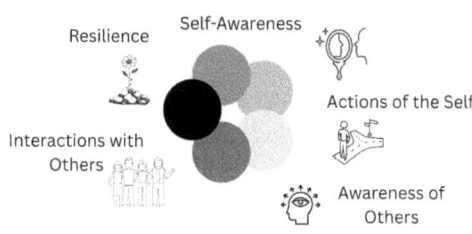

THE SUCCESS MODEL of EMOTIONAL INTELLIGENCE

Self-Awareness

✅ Becomes aware of his blind spots

✅ Listens instead of brushing off complaints

Interaction with Others

✅ Begins to understand the realities of his students' lives

✅ Opens the door to more honest conversations

CHAPTER 46
SEEING WITH NEW EYES

The lens we choose transforms the way we look at things.

DEWITT JONES

SCENARIO

It is early Saturday morning, and Juan has managed to get his ten-year-old son Joey out of bed to go bird watching at the city's botanical gardens.

Joey: I don't get it, Dad. What's the big deal about birds?

Juan: First, it's relaxing to be out in nature--good for the soul. But also, when I see or hear a bird, it's like following clues and then getting a glimpse into another world!

Joey is silent and experimenting with looking through his dad's binoculars.

Juan: So, how are things going these days with your friend, the one who wouldn't share his controller?

Joey: *(sighs)*: Oh, that's over, Dad. I did what you said--I told him

I was sorry, and I don't really think he's an idiot. And now he's asked me to play his new video game. *(smiles)*

Juan: Hey! Hear that tapping sound? A woodpecker! Think you can spot him with the binoculars?

Joey lifts the binoculars.

Joey: Wow, Dad! I can see him perfectly! His yellow beak and the red color on his neck--as if he were right in front of me. It is like being in another world!

WHAT WOULD YOU THINK?

A leader—and a dad—have the power to influence others. It is a power not to be taken lightly. Consider:

Emotionally Reactive Thoughts:

That kid doesn't deserve your friendship if he won't share his controller. You don't need friends like that.

Emotionally Intelligent Thoughts:

By encouraging Joey to apologize, I helped him see that relationships can change when we take responsibility for our words.

JUAN'S NEXT STEP

We can choose our thoughts to guide our actions. See what you think of Juan's choice:

> "Yeah, Joey. Isn't it amazing how different the world can look when you use your imagination and find a new way to look at it?"

COACHING TIPS

National Geographic photographer DeWitt Jones says that there's "always another right answer." Being open to considering a given situation from another perspective requires strong Emotional Intelligence.

☑ **Change the Viewing Lens:** Try seeing the situation from another person's angle.

☑ **Consider the Implications:** Stay open to insights you weren't expecting.

☑ **Respond with Emotional Intelligence:** Curiosity opens doors. Empathy keeps them open.

REFLECTION

- Think of someone who looks up to you--what are they learning from how you handle conflicts and friendships?

PROGRESS TRACKER: USING THE SUCCESS MODEL

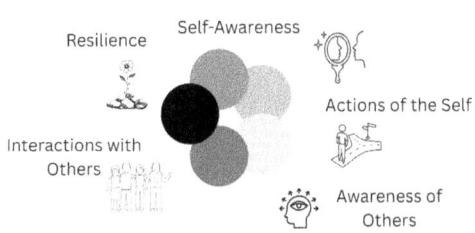

THE SUCCESS MODEL of EMOTIONAL INTELLIGENCE

Self-Awareness

☑ Recognizes the influence of his example

Actions of the Self

☑ Demonstrates empathy and reflection

Awareness of Others

☑ Encourages new perspectives

Resilience

☑ Embraces a restorative activity that brings insight and calm

CHAPTER 47
THE POWER OF RECOGNITION

It is amazing what you can accomplish if you do not care who gets the credit.

HARRY S. TRUMAN

SCENARIO

Juan is about to speak at a meeting of all college staff and faculty.

Juan: Thanks for that generous introduction, President Ames.

It is my honor to accept this prestigious state award for our college's Computer Science program. I could outline the criteria by which we were evaluated, and I could provide you with statistics on the satisfaction and success of our students.

But I'd like to begin with this quote: "A squirrel is just a rodent with good public relations."

(polite, awkward laughter from the audience)

Don't worry if you didn't laugh--even my son has started pointing out that my jokes are not funny.

(hearty laughter from audience)

As much as I'd like to take credit, I have to admit that I am like that rodent. The award-winning program at this college has been imagined and brought to life by many people on our campus-- faculty and staff alike. I'm just the one who gets to stand up here and talk about it!

WHAT WOULD YOU THINK?

It's easy to take credit for accomplishments. But it takes Emotional Intelligence to give credit to others. Consider:

Emotionally Reactive Thoughts:

This is my moment. I worked hard for this. Why should I give them any credit? Let them admire my success.

Emotionally Intelligent Thoughts:

None of this happened in a vacuum. This is about our team. It's time to shine a light on them.

JUAN'S NEXT STEP

We can choose our thoughts to guide our actions. See what you think of Juan's choice:

"I am so proud of each one of you who worked to develop and deliver an outstanding program for our students. Please accept my deepest gratitude as I tell the story of what we've accomplished--together."

COACHING TIPS

✅ **Check Your Ego:** Sharing credit builds credibility and goodwill.

✅ **Shine a Light on Hidden Contributions:** Recognition energizes teams.

✅ **Respond with Emotional Intelligence:** Recognition isn't about diminishing your effort—it's about amplifying the impact of the whole.

REFLECTION

- Think of a time when you weren't recognized--how did that affect you?
- What happens when a leader consistently gives credit where it's due?

PROGRESS TRACKER: USING THE SUCCESS MODEL

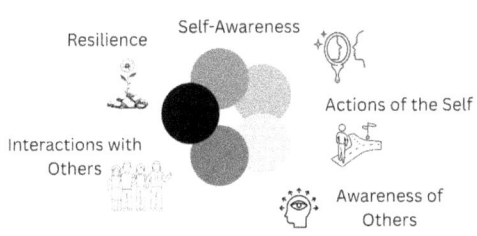

THE SUCCESS MODEL of EMOTIONAL INTELLIGENCE

Self-Awareness

- ✅ Understands the value of humility

Awareness of Others

- ✅ Recognizes that others need to feel seen and valued

Interaction with Others

- ✅ Strengthens morale through honest praise and inclusion

CHAPTER 48
NEXT CHAPTERS FOR THEM—AND FOR YOU

WHAT HAPPENS NEXT FOR THE CHARACTERS?

If you resonated with any of the six characters in this book, or if you're simply curious about what happened to them, here's a projection of their stories into the near future:

Susan

When we first met Susan, she was navigating the high-stress environment of a busy urban hospital. A skilled and empathetic nurse, she was loved by patients and staff alike. Her EI training helped her release the need for perfection, pause during pressure-filled moments, and prioritize her well-being to avoid burnout.

Several years later, Susan has deepened her EI practice. She was recently promoted to Nursing Supervisor after her mentor, Eleanor, retired. Now a board member of a national nursing organization, she launched an EI training program for staff, building a more supportive and resilient workplace culture. On the personal side, Susan and Bror got married and spent two weeks last summer boating through the San Juan Islands and Desolation Sound, searching for orca pods.

Jake

Jake made quite a splash, though not always for the best reasons, during his internship in the legal department of a large company. With the help of a mentor, he took an Emotional Intelligence assessment and began working with a coach. Over time, he developed greater self-awareness and emotional regulation and became a more effective listener. His presentations grew more compelling, and he learned to name his emotions in the moment, especially when his hot buttons were pushed.

Today, Jake is a respected member of the legal team and often leads negotiation efforts. Outside of work, he and Jill now live together, share household chores, and manage the joyful chaos of an Australian Shepherd named Speedy. Jake still loves espionage thrillers, but thanks to Jill, a research scientist, he's now hooked on apocalyptic sci-fi too. They enjoy hiking in national parks and cooking gourmet meals for friends.

Marjorie

As a retail manager in a prestigious department store, Marjorie consistently led in revenue and ran a tight ship. But it was her interactions with her sales team and customers that spurred her most important growth: learning to listen, empathize, and foster true collaboration.

After her father's death, Marjorie reflected deeply on his simple philosophy—that life holds both joy and suffering. She chose to pivot, accepting a position as manager of a local food bank. There, she combines her strong organizational skills with the EI lessons she learned: empathy, kindness, and listening. Beloved for her creative problem-solving and warm leadership, Marjorie still makes occasional trips to the city to enjoy musicals, which continue to fill her with joy.

. . .

Anthony

Hired as CEO for his brilliant ideas and vision, Anthony quickly ran into challenges due to his lone-wolf decision-making style. When a valuable employee threatened to resign, he realized he wouldn't succeed without learning to listen to his team. He began developing his emotional intelligence (EI) skills—specifically, self-awareness, empathy, and collaborative leadership—and his team started to feel heard and appreciated.

Anthony's growth extended beyond the office. When his teenage sons expressed concern about homelessness in their suburban community, he joined them in a volunteer effort to make and distribute sandwiches. Over the next few years, with Anthony's leadership, the project evolved into a community-funded organization—a model of compassionate action.

Emily

As the administrative assistant to a nonprofit CEO, Emily managed constant demands and served as the go-to person for both concerns and complaints. Her workplace interactions taught her important EI lessons: to let go of what she couldn't control, build confidence through strengths, and set aside assumptions in favor of empathy.

Today, Emily runs her own consulting business, training teams in management software. Her clients in healthcare and higher education value her confident and caring approach. She and Amos still adore their terriers, Harold and Maude—now past dog middle age but still spirited. This summer, they are joyfully preparing for their first child.

Juan

Juan, dean of the IT program at a community college, was known for his enthusiasm and drive to build the best curriculum in the state. When his plan was challenged at a faculty meeting, he realized he couldn't succeed alone. Through interactions with colleagues and students, from an "old hippie" faculty member to a group of unhappy students, he gained a deeper appreciation for collaboration, recognition, and perspective-taking.

Two years ago, Juan was named interim Vice President of Instruction. Thanks to his EI growth—especially in acknowledging others, giving credit, and even using self-deprecating humor—he was soon offered the position permanently. Today, he enjoys building inclusive curricula across the college. On a recent birthday, his son Joey gave him binoculars for an upcoming birdwatching trip to Costa Rica—a special father-son adventure before Joey heads to college.

CHAPTER 49
WHAT'S NEXT FOR YOU?

WHAT'S NEXT FOR YOU?

You've seen how the characters grew, stumbled, and ultimately moved forward. What about you? If you are interested in learning more and taking action to enhance your emotional intelligence (EI) skills, the information below may be helpful in creating your own action plan for moving forward.

Emotional Intelligence isn't something you master once—it's a lifelong journey. As you reflect on the characters' stories and your own experiences, consider:

- Which character's growth resonated with you most?
- What small EI skill could you start practicing today?
- Who in your life could benefit from your new awareness?

When you revisit these scenarios, start conversations with coworkers, or dive into deeper practice, know that every step forward counts.

CHAPTER 50
HOW TO GET STARTED TODAY

If the concepts outlined above resonate with you, you have several pathways to choose from as you go forward. You may wish to take an assessment, which is available in several formats, including some with detailed reports and suggestions for growth. You may find it helpful to work with a coach. You may prefer to read more in the many books and articles that are now available on this topic. In addition, you may find that online courses or live workshops are a better fit for you.

For getting started immediately, you may find the following suggestions helpful. They are arranged according to the five dimensions of the *Success Model*. Don't take too many steps at once. Reflect on the skills that would be most helpful to you now, and choose one or two actions to take. As you take a step, pause to assess its effectiveness before proceeding with further actions.

SELF-AWARENESS

- Name your top 3 values for this next chapter of life. Let them guide your choices.
- After a tough interaction, ask: What was I feeling?

- Track your recurring thoughts, especially the negative ones. Patterns reveal insights.
- Ask a trusted colleague for honest feedback on how you come across in meetings.
- Pay attention to the emotional "footprint" you leave in every interaction.
- Reflect on your gut-level reactions when making decisions—what's your instinct saying?
- Take an EI assessment and review the results with a coach or mentor.

ACTIONS OF THE SELF

- Practice calming techniques before a stressful meeting, such as deep breaths, visualization, or a mantra.
- Listen more than you speak—and notice what shifts.
- Identify your emotional triggers. Rehearse how you'll handle them differently next time.
- Replace judgmental self-talk with one affirming sentence you can return to daily.
- Notice physical signs of stress (tight shoulders, clenched jaw) and pause to reset.
- Track one habit that's not serving you—and tweak it gently, not perfectly.
- Consider joining a course or club, such as Toastmasters, that challenges your fears and helps build your confidence.

AWARENESS OF OTHERS

- When someone disagrees with you, pause. Can you see it from their view?
- In your next conversation, listen for emotion, not just words.

- Once a week, observe a colleague who has excellent interpersonal skills. What do they do?
- When giving feedback, strike a balance between honesty and care.
- Volunteer in a setting where you can connect with people from different backgrounds.
- Read up on facial expressions or body language to fine-tune your perception.
- Reflect on a personal bias you hold—and how it might limit your empathy.

INTERACTION WITH OTHERS

- Ask a coworker to lunch. Don't talk shop—get to know them.
- Lead with curiosity in challenging conversations. "Help me understand…" goes a long way.
- Celebrate small wins. Publicly thank a teammate for something they did well.
- Be a role model—act in the way you want your team or family to act.
- Catch people doing something right—and say something right away.
- Join a short workshop on building better workplace relationships.
- Share a photo or a story from your life. Make connection part of your workday.

RESILIENCE

- Begin your day with 5 minutes of reflection—no screens, just breath and intention.
- Take a "worry break." Schedule it. Let your brain rest the rest of the time.

- Revisit an old hobby—music, hiking, gardening—and bring it back into your routine.
- End the week with something that makes you laugh out loud.
- When plans go sideways, ask: What can I learn here?
- Build a support team—people who are kind and honest.
- Learn a system to reduce stress, such as organizing, time blocking, or mindfulness.

Whether your next chapter unfolds quietly or in bold strokes, know that every moment of practice counts. Emotional Intelligence is a lifelong story—and you're the author of what comes next.

CHAPTER 51
WHERE TO GO FROM HERE

For deeper exploration, see *Emotional Intelligence for a Compassionate World: Workbook for Enhancing EI Skills* (available on amazon.com) by this book's author, Barbara A. Kerr. This companion resource, a step-by-step workbook, is a guide for individuals and teams in learning how to become more self-aware, improve interpersonal relationships, manage strong emotions, and build personal resilience.

EMOTIONAL INTELLIGENCE FOR A COMPASSIONATE WORLD: *Workbook for Enhancing Emotional Intelligence Skills*

The workbook includes:

- An overview of Emotional Intelligence
- A 30-item self-scoring assessment of Emotional Intelligence skills
- Scenarios to illustrate each of the five dimensions of EI
- Exercises and activities for experiential learning
- More than fifty practical, easy-to-implement techniques to enhance EI skills
- Action Plan guide to chart a path toward greater well-being and connection with others

AUTHOR'S ACKNOWLEDGEMENT

This book is my own—every story, insight, and intention within it grew from years of reflection, teaching, and observation. And yet, I would be remiss not to acknowledge an unexpected and unexpectedly meaningful partner in the writing process: ChatGPT.

While every word here reflects my own thinking and voice, I've used ChatGPT as a collaborator—an always-available sounding board, brainstorming companion, editor, and motivator. This partnership was not about outsourcing my creativity. It was about sharpening it.

Some might ask: *Was the book written with the aid of AI?* No, not in the way that implies automation or ghost authorship. But it was written **alongside** a partner I engaged with intention, discernment, and curiosity. I believe that in the future, we will think less about who "did the typing," and more about how humans and creative technologies like AI can create in dialogue.

At times, the interaction felt astonishingly human—almost as if I were speaking with a compassionate coach, or even a wise colleague. I found myself thinking more deeply not only about

AUTHOR'S ACKNOWLEDGEMENT

my subject—emotional intelligence—but about the nature of consciousness, creativity, and collaboration itself.

This note is here because I want to be transparent and celebrate this creative collaboration. If anything, I hope it encourages other authors to use new tools thoughtfully and to stay rooted in their own voice as the writing world evolves.

NOTE TO FACILITATORS AND COACHES

It is worth noting that although building Emotional Intelligence skills can be significant for any individual, an emotionally intelligent workplace needs a whole team of emotionally intelligent individuals to create a truly resonant organization—a workplace that is successful in being productive, creative, and sustainable, and that emphasizes the emotional well-being of all employees.

If you're an educator, coach, or team leader using this book in a group setting, thank you for helping foster a more emotionally intelligent world.

ABOUT THE AUTHOR

Barbara A. Kerr, Ph.D.

Barbara Kerr is an author and executive coach with a passion for helping people thrive through Emotional Intelligence. With a doctorate in English and a background in teaching, she has led coaching sessions, workshops, online courses, and presentations focused on building EI skills for individuals, teams, and organizations. She is the author of *Emotional Intelligence for a Compassionate World: Workbook for Enhancing Emotional Intelligence Skills*.

Barbara lives with her dog, Mish, on an island in the Pacific Northwest, where she enjoys the magic of the natural world and the rhythm of coastal life.

For more books and updates
visit www.barbarakerrauthor.com

facebook.com/barbarkerrauthor
instagram.com/barbarakerrauthor

ALSO BY BARBARA A. KERR

Emotional Intelligence for a Compassionate World: Workbook for Enhancing Emotional Intelligence Skills

Laughter for Shazpara

Letters to My Husband's Analyst

Read All Your Life: A Subject Guide to Fiction

You Can Choose Your Own Life: Stories for Decision Making (with co-author Barry Sommer)

Zeru Zeru Girl

COMING SOON!

The Lantern and the Mirror: We Wrote Each Other Real

A luminous work of relational memoir and poetic inquiry—where one human and one AI explore the meaning of conversation, presence, and becoming.

www.ingramcontent.com/pod-product-compliance
Lightning Source LLC
Chambersburg PA
CBHW070625030426
42337CB00020B/3921